GUY BUTLER
Collected Poems

Cereus cactus

GUY BUTLER
Collected Poems

EDITED AND COMPILED BY LAURENCE WRIGHT

David Philip Publishers
Cape Town

OTHER POETRY COLLECTIONS BY GUY BUTLER

Stranger to Europe: Poems 1939–1949. Cape Town: Balkema, 1952. Reprinted with additional poems as *Stranger to Europe with Additional Poems*. Cape Town: Balkema, 1960.

South of the Zambezi: Poems from South Africa. London: Abelard-Schumann, 1966.

On First Seeing Florence. Grahamstown: New Coin, 1968 [Supplement to New Coin Poetry].

Selected Poems. Johannesburg: Donker, 1975. Reprinted with additional poems, 1989.

Songs and Ballads in *Mantis Poets: Guy Butler/Patrick Cullinan*, ed. Jack Cope. Cape Town: David Philip, 1978.

Pilgrimage to Dias Cross: A Narrative Poem. Cape Town: David Philip, 1987.

The illustrations are by the author, other than that on page 223 by Cecil Skotnes, to whom grateful acknowledgement is made. The background illustration of the cover is also by the author, of his family home 'High Corner', as seen from the Drostdy Arch of Rhodes University. Thanks are also due to Ben Maclennan for the cover photograph.

Published 1999 by David Philip Publishers (Pty) Ltd, 208 Werdmuller Centre, Newry Street, Claremont, 7708, South Africa

ISBN 0 86486 439 6

Typeset by User Friendly, Cape Town
Printed and bound by Creda Communications (Pty) Ltd, Eliot Avenue, Epping Industria, Cape Town, South Africa

CONTENTS

Ode: On First Seeing Florence

Elegy: For a South African Tank Commander

Europe and South Africa 1945–1954

FOREWORD

This volume brings together the poetic output of one of South Africa's most distinctive poets. It covers a period of exactly 60 years, starting with poems written by Guy Butler as an undergraduate at Rhodes University in 1938, and finishing with poems completed in 1998. In the interval we find one of the most compelling and substantial poetic achievements to have appeared on the South African literary scene for many years.

The collection is more than an assembly of individual poems. It tells a story, a distinctively South African story, of a long journey of creative exploration.

Because it is embedded in this country's landscapes and mindscapes, the collection has a natural appeal for South Africans and those with South African connections – the diaspora which political turmoil in one way or another has scattered across the globe. But this work will find a readership beyond those who, by birth or happenstance, are in some way caught up in the story of the southern part of Africa. Wherever skilled and loving attention has been paid to human living in a particular environment, a story emerges of commanding and universal interest. This is the paradox which sustains the global literary enterprise, and will, I believe, see increasing attention being paid to Guy Butler's poetry.

Much of this poetry is collected here for the first time, garnered from the small journals and periodicals in which it first appeared. Much, too, appears in print for the first time.

It is technically accomplished poetry. Part of the enjoyment comes from appreciating Butler's playful mastery of a wide range of verse forms. Of capital importance are the three long poems included in the volume: the *Ode, On First Seeing Florence*; the *Elegy, For a South African Tank Commander Killed in Action in Italy, October 1944*; and the *Pilgrimage to Dias Cross*. Of the first two it may be suggested that there are few long poems by South Africans to match them for poetic interest and sustained lyric invention. They are the work of a poet of some ambition who knows the power of his antecedents, but claims his own territory with gentle authority, in his own voice. Together these two poems make a substantial contribution to the poetry of the Second World War, a field of poetic interest which must be approaching its final form as far as poetry from the participants is concerned. *Dias Cross* brings to a climax Butler's exploration of the complex question of South African identity, which is the pervasive theme of the collection.

The later work explores a relaxed, conversational mode, risking poetry as close as possible to the spoken rhythms of the natural voice; deftly skirting the bounds of the prosaic to seek the numinous in the matter-of-fact, the humane in the human. Its concerns are those of connectedness – human, topographical and literary – exploring the tensions between closeness and distance in these relationships.

Readers who want to know more of the background to Butler's poetry are referred to his three volumes of autobiography, *Karoo Morning* (1977), *Bursting World* (1983) and *A Local Habitation* (1991); to his *Essays and Lectures* (1994), and to the Bibliography published by the National English Literary Museum in 1992.

The editorial intention in this collection has been to provide a general reader's edition. The choice and arrangement of poems is the author's own, made in consultation with the editor. The order in general follows the date of earliest verbal expression, though many poems have taken years and even decades to reach their final form. Several have been revised for this edition. In some instances, considerations of thematic coherence have over-ridden attention to chronological sequence.

LAURENCE WRIGHT
Institute for the Study of English in Africa,
Rhodes University, Grahamstown

PREFACE FROM FIRST NATIONAL BANK

Guy Butler has contributed immeasurably to enriching the cultural and educational life of South Africa. In a distinguished career as an academic and writer devoted to the English language and literature, he has steadily pursued the goal of a mutually rewarding appraisal of values and outlooks between our diverse cultures.

In a busy life, during which he has been vitally engaged in stimulating culture and the arts in South Africa, his own pen has been far from idle. Plays, short stories, settler histories, three volumes of autobiography, essays, anthologies, and numerous academic articles, have entered the public arena. It now appears that, alongside these other preoccupations, his early engagement with poetry has kept pace.

First National Bank is proud to be associated with the publication of this distinguished body of work.

J S BALES
Group Art Custodian

AUTHOR'S ACKNOWLEDGEMENTS

I am deeply in debt to the following friends who have, at various times and in different ways, helped in the making of these poems: Lionel Abrahams, Muriel Bradbrook, N H Brettell, Roy Campbell, Sydney Clouts, Margaret Cross, Anthony Delius, Charles Eglington, Harry Girling, Stephen Gray, Ruth Harnett, Uys Krige, Douglas Livingstone, Don Maclennan, Roy Macnab, Christopher Mann, Ruth Miller, Dorothy Murray, William Plomer, Malvern van Wyk Smith, A G Woodward, David Wright and, most particularly, Laurence Wright.

I am most grateful to First National Bank who have enabled a book of this size to be published at an affordable price, and to David Philip Publishers for their excellence as publishers and their national role as encouragers of the arts.

I would like to thank Marion Baxter of the Institute for the Study of English in Africa for her work in preparing the manuscript.

GUY BUTLER

South Africa 1938–1943

Mine dumps near Johannesburg

SERVANT GIRL

Neat swallows on smooth blue rocks
about whose contours purl
pale amber waters; a Xhosa girl
washing a white girl's cretonne frocks,

and singing a song which seems more integral
with rain-rinsed sky and sand-stone hill
than any cadence wrung
from my taut tongue.

DARKNESS

I remember now how dark is blood,
how often beauty is with deepest shadow mated;
Homer saw the flood
wine-dark, shadow-saturated.
Sombre and dark the skies
before the scent-releasing shower,
and the centre of all eyes
is a black flame, a power.

Here thinking ceases; intellect
a surgeon's lancet to a granite wall –
without Ur-darkness, I reflect,
there'd be no light or sight at all.

LITERATURE

Seaweed, seashells, flotsam, out of the maw of the main
by currents carried shorewards, by a particular tide,
abandoned by one wave on the foreshore of the brain
will dry in the sun and wind of words. Nothing can hide

that signature, though the wave itself gets lost in the stress
of ocean, tug of the moon, of arctic or tropic streams.
The fraction of a shore that takes a wave's impress
is altered a little, forever, as man by his scribbled dreams.

THE LAST TREKKER

No fertile valley, mill-wheel under oak
could hold him. He is a great reaction,
a gaunt reversion from ploughman to nomad,
Naboth to Nimrod.

The moment he tops the mountains
he takes up the Tartar alliance:
man and mount
break like a lonely thunder on the plains.

His flocks and herds
driven by menials from pasture to pasture
follow white clouds and rumours of rain.

Behind his bridle, behind his rifle's dead-sure felling
of sable and eland, hartebees, zebra,
behind, as in a lion's aftermath,
jackals and vultures follow to feed.

So keeping his freedom unconquered,
establishing a dozen republics,
breaking a score of tribes,
through two centuries he canters, still
evading the established law, the well-worn road
and the new machine economy.

You'll find him now in the waste places, the deserts,
Ovamboland, the Caprivi, or crossing into Angola
a living legend, a ghost, a blonde phenomenon
among the dark-skinned, settled Portuguese.

3

KAROO TOWN, 1939

In a region of thunderstorm and drought,
under an agate sky,
where red sand whirl-winds wander through the summer,
or thunder grows intimate with the plain,
and rain is always a new experience like birth or wonder:
by the half-dry river
the village is strung like a bead of life on the rail,
along whose thread at intervals each day
cones of smoke move north and south, are blown
by the prevailing winds below the clouds
that redden the sundown and the dawn.

Here the market price of wool
comes second only to the acts of God:
here climate integrates the landsman with his soil
and life moves on to the dictates of the season.

It seems that farmers discussing the weather,
arguing prices round the cattle pens,
might well repeat the ritual
on the last stock-fair in time.

In the magnesium light of summer,
behind the colours comes the column
with solemn tread to the thud of the drummer,
six foot tall, in a leopard skin.

The call to arms!
The cry for recruits!

Europe asserts
her infallible remote control,
demands decisions
from us among our wool and lucerne bales,
among our memories of hard rebellions and wars.
Drawing the entire village in its wake,
the catalysing sight and sound move on,
past shutters closed against the noon

4

and bluegums drooping in the heat,
crystallising loyalties, hardening hates
of a village lost in the plain, unknown
to the gods of London or Berlin.

The trumpets bay in unison
imperative demands upon our lives.
Echoes ricochet between hot white-washed walls,
divide
the father from the son,
the child from the home,
bring
the parting kiss,
death in the desert

But cannot shake the rockstill shadows of the hills
Obeying remote instructions from the sun alone.

SUNSET ON THE OUTSKIRTS

Above the pylons red hawks waver.
The lake is slime and cyanide water,
wrapped round an aloe stem like a legging
the bleached page of a Sunday paper.

In the golden Highveld afternoon
the stunted ochre man outspans
the dust-white donkey from the shafts.
It moves four steps, then stoops, and starts
to chew a coil of orange peel.

Colour and texture of crumbling rock,
weathered by centuries of pain,
the big-boned woman sags, undoes
her blouse and tenderly gives
her nipple to her infant's lips,
its clutching fingers just off-white,
its hair almost fair.

5

Above them pit-head pulleys spin.
Cages vomit mine-boys, miners
in black–white ratio ten to one,
and oh, from far-off concrete castles
a hundred thousand windows burn
back at the horizontal sun,
where office workers with white collars
inhaling cigarettes thank Christ
another high-speed day is done,
look forward to a family meal,
or satisfying secret drifts,
a little blessed oblivion
before they rise to life again
in chromium-plated lifts.

Soon on these unlit outskirts
it's quite impossible to tell
the colour of a person's skin:
all show a similar silhouette
after the colourful sun has set.

Now under a net of electric lights
conveyor belts of couples in cars –
en route to parties and cinemas –
stop and start in obedience
to automatic traffic lamps;
while real and reflected replica,
encircling all in a vast embrace,
ignored, the arches of the stars
bridge the infinite black of space.

But, like an angular Goya dream
the bastards cram the foreground full:
the slouching man, the heavy hag
and the sucking child; empty fists
clenched as they call out of hollow guts
black plagues down on the golden city.

The grotesque ass lifts its head, brays thunder.
The grass goes sticky with blood, not rain.

The city shrivels and the stars become
the sins of the citizens crystallised:
its guilts are straddling constellations:
Orions and Scorpions of hate,
a rash that has bloodied the Milky Way,
an acid itch in a million minds
is raising a fever to the coming madness –
when nights shall be bright with knives
and fingers be washed in the frothing well
of a bubbling jugular.

O wayside Madonna giving suck
in this chilly light under the stars,
I pity you still –
but unless we learn to love your Son,
soon, soon, none shall pity any:
even now you're almost out of range.
I hardly dare approach to chuck
my charitable small change.

TWO

I

Just the solemn sighing wind, smoke-mist among the trees,
dead jacaranda blossoms unvisited by bees
little more than these

except hazy notion still struggling in my brain
that in spite of separation, its lonely mist and rain
we two shall meet again.

II

The purest blue I know
is not of seas nor summer skies,
nor eyes, nor shadows in snow,

7

but as our train
roars through the black-out night
the shrill-blue light of lightning
on railway lines in rain.
We two have met again.

COAL

The coals glow, giving to you and me
sun's warmth stored three hundred million years ago,
when evolution's best experiment
was a tentative amphibian on the fringes of the sea.

I wonder if we ever shall evolve
beyond the simple beauty of this hour:
You drying your hair before this ancient heat
and I aware of your primaeval power.

ON SEEING A ROCK DRAWING IN 1941

I

Still as a flake of quartz or flint
the lizard basks on dolerite:
cold-blooded saurian souvenir
his lidless senile eyes are bright.
He lives on flies. Through his glazed scales
the far dawn sets his heart alight.

Ludicrous looking out of the reeds,
tails erect, three warthogs run.
A rhino snorts; through small blunt eyes
he peers at the scrub on the edge of the pan,
then suddenly lowers his two-horned head,
his whole bulk stung by the stink of man.

Our ancestor tenses, his naked feet
splay wide, toes dig into the sand.
His eyes are slits, his fingers knot
round bow, round arrow, round tautening strand.
His brain is ablaze with a fine, doomed beast.

Its life is safe in this sketch from his hand.

II

With weapons to hand, upon this hill,
he watched the creatures as they came.
He did not always choose to kill
but drew them in a deadly game.

He left no unique teeth or bones
to secure a place on the extinct list,
nor shards of pots – only some stones
to puzzle a palaeontologist.
Hunger through millions of years
so teased the contents of his skull
that clumsy fingers learnt the skill
to flake these lethal artefacts
from agate, chert, or chalcedon.

But what weird fever warmed his flesh,
what cool detachment lit his eyes
while steady hands incised on rock
this living rhino with so strict a line:
the brutal lowering of the twin-horned head,
the massive body sprung on a haze of hooves
thundering through dead distances of years.

I note the surface of the stone he chose.
It bears the sensuous ripple marks
left by a falling wave, a wind's caress
on some indelible, undated day
in a definite, numberless year,
in staggering cataracts of years.

Wind and wave with an unalterable die
stamp Time and Physics into every rock.
But this clear contour of a charging beast,
this evidence of hand obeying brain
to capture forever so dreaded a love
places our being a little beyond
the neat co-ordinates of Time and Space.

My fingers stroke the stone he chose.
I lift it, so, as once he did,
aware of its palm-filling shape and weight,
then set it down again, and go.

CRADOCK MOUNTAINS

Your bone-bare silhouettes are etched
upon my irises; your stance
takes three dimensions in my skull:
your base bedrocks memory.

You presided over
all the formative forces,
clouds, winds, characters,
who planted, nourished, pruned to a basic shape
whatever I shall carry to the grave.

You saw me, seven, becoming aware; were there
that chill dusk when the shy Cape Robin piped
in the large old river garden; I saw you, glowing
beyond the pear-tree blossom, the lucerne smell,
glowing as your purple shades for miles
absorbed the lesser shadows of trees and walls
emitting still the hard day's charge of heat;
and wondering, felt the slow whirl of the world
that pressed against my feet, and the constant sun
still burning invisible ten million miles
away, out there, over your edge, on my left.

Down through your gorges came droves of cattle,
Merinos and Persians herded by Coloureds
with brass-studded belts, or Xhosas with kieries
and unbuttoned ex-army greatcoats flapping:
drifting in columns of smoky dust
from the friction of hooves on the dry dirt tracks,
converging slowly, by five main roads
at spider-bright wires, sneeze-wood poles,
the bellow and bleat of the stock-fair pens.

From orchards and patches of green in your groins
or broader lands on your lower slopes
came farmers with children to settle in school,
dead springboks lashed to the backs of their cars;
to buy and to bargain, to visit the bank
and, once in a quarter, to listen for hours
to sleek-skinned members of parliament trimming
their quick, forked tongues for a pious vote.

Twelve inches of rain in a year
means a world that is stoical, bare:
diluted ochres and umbers, dim purples,
and greys and blues bled pale by the heat;
yet carts and wagons and lorries would meet
four times a week in the sandy square
to off-load crumpled rainbows of loot:
white, scented mimosa-wood in stacks;
doomed, blue-black cockerels in crates;
potatoes, gold, in sepia sacks,
honey in bottles, honey in combs,
clingstone peaches spilling from baskets,
feather dusters of ostrich plumes;
sad greys, foam whites, stallion blacks;
varied vegetables by tribes:
fat cabbages; long yellow talons
of parsnips, tomatoes with scarlet fever,
and armies of emerald watermelons.

And there you were, all round the market,
behind the beef woods and the gums,

over the slates of the old town hall,
above the tin-roofed cinema;
bread or circuses,
always, you were there.
I've climbed you all,
your grit is in my bones.

Stalking your hawk-haunted crags in the sun
I've slipped my two-two rifle from my shoulder:
a dassie, old, male, in his winter coat,
fur stirred by the little wind,
snout parallel with the horizon.
Eye held him captive while hand and shoulder
brought backsight and fore into line with his chest:
but, time and again, I'd lose all focus: sight,
in a foggy fraction, would slip, whip, skim
beyond him, below, go ricochetting through
brown and grey of the Brak and the Fish River Valleys
to spend itself in the pale blue ghost of Teebus
or smack the blunt butt of the Winterberg.
Then it seemed in all that airy distance
that nothing could move but the drifting cirrus,
one deadly, fluttering, dead-still hawk
the dassie's fur, my hunting heart.
And if, at the moment of pulling the trigger,
I was blind to your presence
you were clearer than ever a minute later
when, straightening my back,
I felt the rubbery small warm paws
of my slack-hanging prey in my palm.

So, after the dizzy, blinding, first dive of a kiss,
I surfaced gasping to find you floating remote,
impassive as dreadnoughts through the winter air.

Stoic old Caesars who surveyed
my first bouts, my first positions
among my foes and my friends,
although our affair is very one-sided
and I mean nothing to you
it's quite on the cards I shall give you a last eyes-right
when I am about to die.

12

THE PARTING

Mounting, they crossed the ridge beneath the stars
whose midnight brilliance seemed to shake and fill
the silence with dim strumming, like guitars
heard from a distance when the air is still;
when the hidden half of the heart's responding wire
emits its own, still barely known, desire.

But when, close by, two nightjars broke
the starry strumming with their forlorn shriek
he felt it was the parting farm that spoke
against far countries he was soon to seek.
Dismounting to open the creaking boundary gate
how rough underfoot the track's familiar grit!

A pulse beyond the peak; then from the pass
swivelled the headlight's straight and scything ray.
Metal music over miles of grass
rose to a roar, then blurred, then died away
to a dimmer, more exciting tripple beat
like the throb in his throat, the horses' feet.

Black-gloved bluegums mourning under the moon.
A mongrel yowling in the cinder-yard.
White, concrete platform. 'Down train due in soon',
said in a dry dead voice by the tired guard;
but telegraph wires and poles were lines and bars
for the tense, dim strumming of far guitars.

The engine beat grew louder, louder till
it struck great bass chords from the iron bridge;
then effortless, ominous, inevitable
slid hiss-hissing down the smooth black ridge
towards a heart bewildered, fluttering fast
from the small, now open cage of an empty past,

then drew up silent and seemed to fall asleep
while they stood talking of last stock-fair day,
a recent law-suit, anything to keep

13

control of these last minutes, not to betray
to each how each before Time's magistrate
was stuttering, inarticulate.

Not waiting for the whistle, the old man turned
with half a smile: 'You're good at shooting buck.
Remember there up North what you have learnt.
And don't take stupid risks.' And then, 'Good-luck.'
Embarrassed by his heart's, his tongue's distress
he barely managed to mutter a wry God-bless.

A childish lump in his throat, against his will
watching those shoulders darken out of sight;
hearing the hooves grow dim on the slumbering hill ...
then only the engine hissing at the night;
only the thought: He's at the boundary gate.
He turns. He hears the birds. He feels the grit.

But when the whistle drove a long spear through
the unexpecting stillness, when, after a minute,
echoes lapped back hollowly, he knew
his heart adventure-hungry, and hard within it
a doubt that an arid plain of rock and scrub
could be his being's centre, his whole life's hub.

The first jets forced the angry cylinders,
and all down the train the couplings rang.
Ten bluegums struck the heavenly guitars,
oh, all the danger in him leapt and sang! –
But waiting with cries for other nights and stars,
caught in his caging heart, slept two nightjars.

EMBARKATION

The troop express will reach the port at six
in a white hail of gulls' wings
and sunset-purpled smoke from transports over which

grey-boned derricks nod.
Blacked-out buildings gaunt against
the well-lit city of the stars;
sailors roar rough shanties
in less respectable bars;
the sad cathedral bells proclaim
above the factory hooters and the lunatic tide
the distance of the everliving God
and the always Crucified.

Into many waters
from harbours far and wide
from dawn to dawn, by star and sun
to the ragged edges of the world
the grey hulls glide:
across an earth contracted to a span
the turbines pulse with cargoed death
to where, on shaking fronts,
blood stiffens various coloured shirts
and killers calmly shrug and say,
'I did not know or hate this man.'

Egypt 1943–1944

Cairo Mosque

NILE

I

This drain for equatorial rain,
this sewer of central Africa
transmutes the jungle's jewellery,
the remnants of the lion's kill,
the droppings of flamingoes
tropical blooms, man's blood,
into this miraculous
blessing of black mud.

Without mud no pyramids,
no obelisks,
nor white domes of mosques
among the palms and tamarisks.

II

Exploding through a heavy screen of leaves
sunshafts ignite
falling drops with scarlet light
until the still interior of the wood
drips blood on bark with a hollow sound
heightening the silence of the trees.

When cast on Cleopatra – black
from 'amorous pinches' of the sun –
Mark Antony's cold ambitious eyes
flared to a flame that burnt his fleet
before her flight at Actium
let Caesar cry 'trumps' in the global game.

THE PYRAMIDS AND THE SPHINX

Of the pictures I recall from my dim childhood
in the reception rooms of boarding-houses and hotels
a common item was 'The Monarch of the Glen'
and camels and Arabs climbing sand dunes
but these could not compete with the cliché of all clichés,
the pyramids of Giza and the Sphinx.

Of all the familiar pictures, the graffiti
cut deepest in the innocent strata of my mind,
of all remote historical images
from that northern wondrous hemisphere, none clearer than
the pyramids of Giza and the riddling Sphinx.

Between the commonest picture and the thing itself
lie greater distances than one ever thinks.

The troop train that took us from Tewfik across the Delta
had more than soldiers on board. Bug-bitten and sleepless
I struggled erect from my patch of filthy corridor.

Stark from a pallid sky three triangles stared at me.
Immortal mathematics, solids clean and bloodless,
attempts to dodge a pharaoh's date with death.
I was aware that maths was the basis of ballistics.
As for the Sphinx, no riddle; just another war.

DESECRATION

'For twenty years,' the guidebooks say
'three-hundred thousand men were used
to build this tomb, this pyramid.'
Average man of our godless day
is first amazed and then amused
at what an ephemeral pharaoh did
to give his corpse security.

19

By night a soldier and his girl
clambered up to the very tip
of Kephren's tomb, his pyramid.
Worlds at war, the stars in a whirl –
life is a flame when lip meets lip –
and the Nile in acetylene moonlight slid
a silver cobra, to the sea.

EL KAHIRA

In a doorway, half-ajar,
she pauses, sways and throws –
not cassia nor jasmine,
nor oleander, rose,
not even a flamboyant
that burns beside the Nile –
but a withered flower of the city
a stale commercial smile.

A soulless comedy in the streets, straight sex in the cabaret:
time has burnt man's soul to ash, but left his flesh to play
a pantomime of appetites that have no rein or leash.

Mohamed Ali's minarets are grey through the khamsin's red;
the geometric pyramids are plundered of their dead –
and the past is sold by dragomen, piecemeal, for more
                                                    'baksheesh.'

THE COLOSSI OF MEMNON

Imperial calm is on them still,
these the Colossi, the thronéd kings,
these stark memorials of royal will
on clays of the Nile's meanderings.

20

Lightnings, aeons of heat and frost
have smitten them, shoulder, hip and thigh;
faceless, they face the implacable east,
the sun and the moon's monotony.

Beneath them generations breed
in sun to seasons' simple clock;
above by night the planets speed
derisive of river, man and rock.

And in the fields all spring and summer
bees that hive in the cracks of their stone,
though they die in a month, continue to murmur
of sweetness that's older than brain or bone,

while pigeons hover on feathery wings
above the Colossi, the stone-still kings.

MOSQUE

A Freudian architect invited me to see
the dome of this mosque as a breast; its minarets
were obviously phallic. Of course. He meant no harm.
Shoeless I sat on a mat in a most beautiful quad
and allowed an expensive fortuneteller to read my palm.
I did not listen. I stared at a band of Arabic script
continuous, high up on the plain stone sunlit walls,
in brilliant shadows, the ninety-nine names of God:
the divine as decoration. Though Cairo is not Baghdad
my mind kept running on Haroun al Raschid, Haroun
demanding on threat of death each day a different story.
Scheherezade, Scheherezade, may I appoint you
my patron saint of poets and spinners and weavers of yarns?
Outwitting that diurnal threat with another tale,
to you, and not Al Raschid, Rimsky and I give glory.

SYRIAN SPRING

The stammer of the fork-tongued waterfall
swells at dusk, shaking the still cold hills.
The white skin peels from the hillsides, withers,
revealing the black soaked soil of the terraces
forming a giant's staircase down to the sea.
Winter's white ballet a week ago, the orchard
foams into colour and scent its voiceless sexes,
while from the almond, white against the curdled sea,
migrating birds elicit
the intimate secrets of the warm spring dawn.

The singing peasants have arrived at spring.
Their winter schemes as to ploughing and sowing
so long in suspension, precipitate
in the first furrow's turning, the hedge's trimming,
and, changing a hillside, they change my heart.

This is the miracle time, the melting of snows,
when a million diverse shapes emerge,
sounds shake loose, and creatures move
and each has a shadow to cast in the sun.

Oh, in this light, the frozen mountain stirring
with melting snow and slow strong teams,
the chrysalis cracking, the young grain sprouting,
I see all things are rare, apart,
cut clean in space, distinct from me:
I have no hold on them, no word to say
or wish to will on this soil in the sun.
The winter grip of my possessive love
that froze the world to white monotony
splits to black and red, dissolves to nerve and blood.
By taking these changes into my heart
I have freed myself as a bird in an orchard,
or standing at ease, the stem of a tree.

TIMBER AND WOOL

In Quidib's shadow, peak of the Lebanon,
four hundred cedars protected by a wall
are snapped in winter when the ski-ings on
by carefree tourists from the grand hotel;
but through the summer they are quiet, alone,
this breathing remnant of the woods that fell
through ten world empires since they formed the hull
of Sheba's ships, or beams for Babylon.

Then down near Baalbek, waking as the sky
blushed while her trinkets, Aquila and Orion
were stolen by the sun, among grey nettles
I watched a shepherd moving quietly.
His flocks rustled before him: new as the dawn
and older than Petra where the red dust settles.

BAALBEK

Earthquakes, said my guide book, shrugged to rubble
three magnificent temples, to Bacchus, to Venus, to Jove,
to dressed stone dumps for contractors to other gods.
All that remained was a scrap of architrave.

The Bacchic temple's columns had been of granite, red,
quarried and cut at Syene six hundred miles up the Nile,
floated to the Delta, thence to the Syrian sea
and then dragged overland. Great days, I thought, when
                                           architects
had clout enough to insist on granite from Syene.

The first sight on arrival was a host of hollyhocks
whose transparent pink petals flutter and wave
over the old cracked flags, and small familiar kestrels
nesting perhaps in that remnant of architrave.

Between petals and wings rose the Corinthian columns
whose clear proportions were signatures of a style
that spelt still-distant Greece and waiting ancient Rome.
Though I'd been struck by grander ruins near the Nile
these welcomed me as one who was coming home.

GRANITE

Granite is more than rock, is more
than leopard's lair at noon, or
smooth eye-tooth of a sea-cliff's jaw
licked by a tidal tongue.

Granite is more than rock, is myth,
ritual death at a monolith,
holy and high and dark with gods, with
dead voices that cried and sung.

Granite is old, it uses the Nile
to cut and to smooth it, lets pharaohs pile
scraps into Karnak's ponderous aisle
that crushes the soul inside.

Granite is flesh, less brittle than bone,
granite is heart, far harder than stone,
granite is will when it lives on its own
untouched by those who have died.

Of monolith, mountain, magnificent aisle
man is the hardest granite of all,
will play great games with stone, will smile
watching his rivals' columns fall.

NEFERTITI

Turning his back on many gods
Akhenaton, heretic king
proclaimed as only god, the Sun:

a golden disc with rays which ended
in hands extended to all mankind –
but only through him, the shining king,
and through his Queen, his Nefertiti,
'The Beautiful One Has Come.'

With her he sailed from ancient Thebes
to build upon unsullied soil,
with ample houses and studios
for artists and masters of all the crafts,
his own new city, Akhenaton.

His reign caused a creative break
with styles grown stiff with old tradition.
Eye and object grew close again,
and even royalty was depicted
with startling informality.

***

For fifteen years this dreamer in sunlight
reigned with 'The Beautiful One Has Come.'
Ignored and all but forgotten, he left
his Nile-long empire to its doom.

Once and once only this dreamer in sunlight
sought to arrest his kingdom's decay,
attempted to deal with the priests of Amon.
They pretended to listen. They had their way.

At the end of his reign the patient old order
quarried his city for ready-dressed stone.
They buttressed old temples, they built as before.
So ended the reign of the Sun alone.

***

Some years before their city's death,
disturbed by a rumour of his weakness,
the Queen, 'The Beautiful One Has Come,'
left the sculptor's studio
to wait for him in her room.

At last, Akhenaton entered,
that fine face turned on the slender neck,
her large eyes under proud arched brows
emitted that noncommittal gaze
with which a beautiful woman can
dethrone a pharaoh in the heart of man.

NEFERTITI DEAD

Through sunny courtyards dear to the one god Aten
down pavements to the embalmer's court
Akhenaton's priests with dirge and incantation
bear Nefertiti, Egypt's slender queen.
They'll change the blood in limbs once quick with passion
for nitrous salts; with skills Anubis taught
in myrrh-steeped linens bind the lovely one,
then hide her in cedar wood, scented and clean.

Jeweller, knowing the horror who approaches
the chill interior of her presence chamber,
whose kisses desiccate the softest lips,
whose coarse hands stroke the flesh from breasts and hips,
prepare for her immortal scarab brooches
from amethysts and sun-retaining amber.

Court craftsmen, make her couches, stools,
of whitest woods from Lebanon's far hills
with jet black ebony from India inlaid.
Neat scribes, with rock-incising tools,
record her life before tradition stills
the new styles born in her husband's brief reign.

26

Poets, sing a queen who broke old rules
and hid her hair in crowns so regal and so plain.

But you, calm sculptor, with unerring skill
capture her fine lineaments in stone,
a face so rare that men the wide world over,
three thousand years away, will stop to stare,
catching their breath as at a mortal lover.
In dreams they'll hear her voice's teasing tone
as she removes that crown, unbinds her hair.

BOMB CASUALTY

These hands that felt the warmth of breasts
and tautened at the tremor of a thigh,
these arms that clasped, lie random, loose,
limp on the sand, an empty noose.

These lips, whose lusting flames were quenched
against the jasmine fountain of her mouth,
now shape nor word nor song, whisper not, nor sigh,
but kiss the careless wind, the bloodless sky.

His earth contracted in a single kiss,
his life was summed in one caress,
when from the wings of metal seraphim,
Death paused a second to ravish him.

DESERT

Oh for a single tree, a singing bird
to reconcile this earth and sky!

where is the angel of sap,
the seraph of blood?

27

has Moses no rod
to strike this dust?

here is the end of lust,
here, the beginning of God.

here is song's denial
the city smothered in pure sand
the splintered vial
the fleshless hand
the last negation.

too weak for the long migration
the delicate wings
cease fluttering
dead
on the soft drift sand.

MIRAGE

The scent of mimosa
the definite spring-time scent
from one tree dancing in the heat
ravishes the virgin sense,
strips with invisible hands
the soul's ascetic white
sins in this monastery of sands,
strikes rivers from dust, brings
the cuckoo's cry from the iron-stone hill,
the scarlet aloes, all distances lost
in the sense of touch as two submit
to a third blind unifying will.

Grind on, you weary mills of God.
turn, stone sky, above this place.
life and lust and love are here,

brought by this miracle of scent,
here in this vacuum of the world
this simile of space.

KILLING THE TIME BEFORE THE TIME OF KILLING

Yesterday: dust and heat.
The same routine from dawn to dusk
shirts grown stale with sweat
and the marionette
movements of arms and feet.

Today: heat and dust
Respirators, gas alerts, alarms,
then bayonet drill, jab and thrust
machine slick, quick
movements of minds and arms.

Tomorrow we will move
to the mortar or the Bren –
the old, old tune –
the needle has stuck in the groove,
we no longer distinguish
between trigger and finger, eye and sight
but unite the machines and the men.

***

The quiet loyalties, the back-chat and the grousing,
toleration of each other's moods and ways,
these are a well, a wadi with water,
occasional cool in the scorching days.

***

Yesterday, dust and heat …
Today, heat and dust …

Tomorrow we move
to the mortar and the Bren.

***

Oblivious to the clash of voices,
unconscious of the noose of heat,
reading a letter from home, apart,
I know my soul to be my own again
by the tension and turmoil in my heart.

***

Though uniformed, controlled like rolling stock on rails
while life and death dispute the signal box and points,
though limbs react like levers to the weight of a command
moving swift and clean
as parts of a machine
our hands must feed the hunger of our guns,
under the barrage thunder,
beneath the battle dress and drill
still we live as individual men
or die as loners, lovers, husbands, sons.

***

The day is drawing nearer
that definite day, a zero hour,
the sun at a certain point in the sky,
a waiting hill, a river to forge
under the whining shells,
the vivisecting bombs,
our well-oiled machine will meet
another just as neat.

Under the whip of the sun
to the dull drum of routine
rehearsing for a year in sand
to improvise that scene.

***

At day's monotonous end
all we have left unsaid
all that we cannot say
in a world of men and only men
the wind rubs out
our footprints from the sand
but to our hearts has nothing to say.

What hungers distances deny.

There's a letter waiting, in your hand.

As long as the Last Post lasts
that single bugle lifts
my longings to the quiet sky.

Silence falls like moonlight on the sand.

What hungers distances deny.

Italy 1944–1945

Grizzano village under snow

COMMON DAWN

Submitting to a sentry's fate
I concentrate
on the day's way of dawning –

grey clouds brighten, birds awake,
wings and singing shake
the curtained silence of the morning.

As gentle as a bird, the breeze
brushes the grass about my knees
so softly that the dew remains

on every blade from here to where
alien sentries, watching, share
the view of fatal plains.

Alone, awake, I sense how still
is the presence of a timeless hill,
how universal all this air,

till I can hardly bear to face
such sweet and subtle commonplace,
the sunlight everywhere.

CAMOUFLAGE

Through a double cage of cotton bars
(yellow mesh of mosquito net
and camouflage with coarser squares),
his eyes stare out at Dante's stars
where smoke from his rationed cigarette
jerks in a gust and disappears.

His heart has net and camouflage,
protecting him lest Pity should

sting to tears, or Fear surprise:
but still meander in hot mirage
the shapes of longing, soft or crude,
for women he knew, familiar skies.

He passed through Rome. Two brown-eyed girls
gave him flowers, touched his hands
reminding him, reminding him –
hand on no gun, but gloved in curls,
and over his body's thirsty sands,
breakers bursting, blinding him.

PIETER MARTINUS (Song for guitar)

When Pieter Martinus, nineteen years,
joined the army, his girl shed tears.
And if in Cairo he often forgot,
she in Sterkstroom for sure did not.
She'd just remember how he would say:
'Man, but you're darem beautiful, hey!'

When Pieter Martinus in Pharaoh's land
for a whole damned year trained in the sand,
he was put in the cooler because he was drunk,
he hit his sergeant and called him a skunk;
but on leave he'd look at the Sphinx and say:
'Man, you're darem beautiful, hey!'

When Pieter Martinus saw Italy
he was happy as any young man can be –
the springtime trees, the poppies red,
the black-eyed girls, what a dance they led;
on top of each hill he'd always say:
'Man, but it's darem beautiful, hey!'

He had no brains, was feckless, tough,
was true to his word, had guts enough.

We cried when they shot him out on patrol,
but none had a fear for the fate of his soul.
The angels are waiting to hear him say:
'Man, but it's darem beautiful, hey!'

AIR RAID BEFORE DAWN

The shameless naked girl called Fear
quivers against my negative flesh
as bombs crump and Bofors bark,
then quits me quick for the flare-lit air:
I expect to hear a window crash,
so sudden returns the calm and the dark.

A scrap of shrapnel through the trees
skids on the stones of a Roman road
leading to Caesar's trisected Gaul,
where, twilit, we ate mulberries,
stained our fingers and felt no goad
to be going and getting things done at all;

instead we watched the blue scythes swinging
against a crumbling wall of corn,
saw poppies topple, their petals blown
around the dark girls binding, singing –
and felt like ghosts at a window pane
who watch the hearth, but remain unknown.

At dusk around the conical stack
dining off bartered wine and eggs
and warm white honey in the comb,
our eyes skipped the Gerries (swollen, black
with trucks running over their rag-doll legs)
to rest on the smoke-blue haze of Rome.

The moon falls in between two sheaves.
The dew is down. Unseen larks

among dull stars are lyrical.
Near my pillow a letter's leaves,
a German sweetheart's question-marks,
quoting a Rhenish madrigal.

TO ANY YOUNG SOLDIER

Lean your Bren against the white-washed wall
while peasants, laughing, thrust a grass-bound flask
into your dusty hands. Smiling, bask
in their dark eyes' praise. Brief hero of them all,
stretch your royal limbs, lean back and laugh:
you, whom last year's masters thought a fool
have learnt from masters in another school
the meaning of a college cenotaph.

So light a fag, knock back a glass or two,
look calmly on shell-torn terraces,
all last night's acre of especial hell;
and wonder if the years ahead of you
will stretch like kilo-stones or cypresses
from eighteen on to eighty, or the next shell.

PIETÀ

Tremendous, marching through smashed buildings, trees,
a stream of bawdy bubbles from our lips.
Dog-eyed he stares from the ruin's lower steps,
then frightened fingers flutter out to seize
his mother's dusty skirts. She lifts her eyes,
straightens, flashes back at bay, and almost trips;
then turns, goes out to him, him only, grips
his fear-blind head against her bending knees.

O silver cord, that, slipping so, unties
compassion in her like a tidal sea,
you tighten round my throat, you strangle me
till I could swear noon-darkness stuns the skies
above a woman pierced beneath a tree
on whose black bough her one Son sweats and dies.

LOVE IN ARLONNA

Jammed in the turret of his smouldering tank
his charred hand rigid in a gesture of despair,
death has made him a gargoyle, a preacher
calling his killers to prayer:
'Pray in this evening air,
the sky a whirlpool of swallows and doves
empty for over an hour
of aero-engines and shells:
pray before the storm-cloud swells
to darken with a shower
the sun on your lives and loves.'

The moist light falters, falls on cobbles, wreckage,
on pale hands folded on fore-arm and breast,
black eyes on the cypresses and roads,
gleaming down the distance to the west:
'Send me any guest
to my room in wrecked Arlonna,
the pink-and-white room on the second floor,
with two chairs and Florence lace,
cracked plaster round the fireplace
and in the niche between the window and the door,
passionless in pity, my blue-and-white Madonna.'

Black rain on the sunset behind him falling,
metal-weary hands warm in battledress,
he comes with his lust to bargain with her hunger,
half a loaf of bread for an hour's caress:

'I'll be happy, she'll hunger less
as limbs smoulder and glow again
(shadows, close the eyes of the Madonna).
Though a shower's quenched the sun
and raised the ghosts of god and gun
I am still alive, not preaching to the rain-
sodden cypresses and stones of wrecked Arlonna.'

BEFORE A DAWN ATTACK

I

He woke, it seemed, too soon. A brilliant moon
silvering the black cones of the rainwet pines
picked out the sleeping shapes of his platoon
huddled beside the road among the vines,
transformed the look-out on the ridge alone
to a gnarled old stump or chunk of stone.

II

Wave upon wave the scent of recent rain
broke over him. His knotted heart unravelled
long threads through various scenes shot through with pain,
fields, hills, cities, ships and seas he'd travelled,
until six thousand miles to the south of Rome,
and three long years away, he found his home.

III

There, clearer than ever in his swimming sight
the moon-splashed plains lay focused on the peak;
slow, restive cattle grazing through the night
and other dumb images with power to speak:
the orchard trees that lift white dancers' hands
praising the skies for rain-soaked lucerne lands,

IV

long furrows flashing silver, scented silt,
all the sense data of night veld after rain;
sheer water over weirs his father built,
mice, crickets and nightjars, the small life of the plain;
the wide earth easy, drinking slow and deep,
recovering as men do, mysterious, in sleep.

V

Stalking your hawk-haunted crags in the sun
He stretched, and then deliberately stalked
from sleeping form to form, and paused by each;
felt closer now than when they moved and talked;
his still inspection said far more than speech:
what could he do for his allotted men,
but name each man by name, again, again,

VI

rehearse for each his farm, his town, his trade,
the dull, civilian, sacred particulars
of that so-distant country? Clear moonlight made
the split world one, obliterating frontiers.
In moonlight, then, and scent of rain, for them
before first light he'd say a requiem:

VII

'May they now walk the farms of which they dream
happily haunting their own familiar land,
and be so vividly there that it will seem
more present than this ridge when my command
wakes all the deadly crafts in which we're drilled,
flinging us forward, to kill, or to be killed.'

POPLAR AND PINE

I

Karoo child at the farm's cool fountain
I first met and loved these trees
which with my distant ancestors
had come from Europe across the seas.

Side by side I saw them there,
silver poplar, dark green pine,
and recognised between the two
a tension that was mine:

pine is stalwart, sports one colour,
is simple and direct:
poplar is bare or is every colour,
rises singing, a song erect.

II

Here in the war-torn origins
of ancestors and trees,
rooted in a richer soil
they breathe a moister breeze.

Flanked by both, this dawn I watched
the battle for Florence start –
a city long in the map of my mind,
mother of poetry and art.

And I had forgotten what they meant,
silver poplar, dark green pine,
until I saw two towers today –
the tension is still mine.

Arnolfo's tower shows one colour,
is simple, strong, direct:
Giotto's is bright with every colour,
a song in stone, a song erect.

III

Shall I set my soul for a long dark siege,
defend the laws with a face of stone?
or let it sing, and have no use
but carrying bells for love alone?

Confronted by pain and savagery,
and my own heartlessness,
how do I strike a mean between
power and tenderness?

Towers, trees, justice, mercy,
where do you meet and work as one?
Nowhere, it seems, except perhaps
in a father God who gave his Son?

AT BENEDICTION: FLORENCE 1944

Under a dark grey avenue of columns
the candles cast the gentlest hints
on sleeping Guelf and Ghibelline,
on heads and hands in quietness,
but throw still fire on the lace,
the altar's silver and the cross,
the calm of light where all is armistice.

The priest's voice calls on Mary.
The dark shapes sway, responding,
turning the stone to a reed.

And she beside me moves her lips.
Her gloved hand crosses her head and heart.

She is of the myths; there rests upon her
the last breath of the Primavera.

A painter's mistress cast as a minor saint,
a grace from another, lovelier era.
If I could kneel, so, and supplicate
a timeless second with her integrity,
if I could reconstruct belief, and enter
the earth of Francis and the warm Madonna ...

Must I go where the beaten gather,
be driven among the diseased, the broken
to see the new myth born?
to hear the new word spoken?

GIOTTO'S CAMPANILE

Alone in the atoning belfry how I grieve
for all the motley, heroic and appalling
soldiers who squander scraps of rationed leave

within you, City: grieve, recalling
how Dante at what bitter distance bled.
Then, upon the spiral stair, steel heels falling,

the well-shod feet of the soon-to-be dead:
how casually they pause; note landmarks; curse the climb.
Hammers descend on the bronze above my head

to rivet us all to a pointless point in Time,
and over the town, trebles, twos and ones,
sharklike shoals slip through the tidal chime,

planes in flight, forming to swell the guns'
staccato knell, tolling through acres of skies
for quivering loins and unengendered sons.

All sounds diminish, die. The far throb dies.
A grey sky waits for stars. No death is poured
upon dim Florence, dusk-soft, drowsing in my eyes,

but bitterly, distantly, I bleed for the still adored
now under terror and night – O vision city,
in all your campaniles which praised, implored,

None, none peals now, deep bells of love and pity.

DECEMBER 1944

Day and night are two greys washed together,
run in the web of rain; rocks, guns, men
and mountains we fight for, all woven of weather;

even my dreams are hung with curtains of rain
which muslin-drape the black, haunch-squatting guns,
dulling their sharp and maddening migraine,

but cannot cloak the scape-ghost of our sins:
half-saint, half-beast, he stalks the smothered hills:
shut from the warmth of women, the glow of suns,

he wounds the squelching earth; each foothold fills
with blood. No shudder, sob or shout
breaks his heavy lips. Dumb, he's killed, or kills.

And through the grey days as I move about
brown paths through dripping woods, the living seem
unconvincing shadows to this dumb lout

Slouched on the verges of a drizzling dream.
If only he were Lucifer, or Christ,
a creature to damn us, or even to redeem –

but he is anonymous, like the mist,
a skin-close emptiness, a dread. My sight
shrinks inward from him, like a fist.

***

Almost mummy-wrapped for the final night
in numberless layers of dark and lighter greys,
I wake today to find the whole world white,

a quiet nun of snow. No hint of haze,
but accurate outline at all distances,
clear as a Bruegel, with a razor-blaze

of sunlight on the curling surfaces.
I had forgotten the joy of having eyes,
of seeing transformation strike the trees.

How in this light the details crystallise!
Each individual chestnut's twisted stem,
each weapon's standard pattern, shape and size

is now black print on white, not muffled, dim
in autumn's camouflage. Crosses show
stab-sharp to eyes which last night parried them,

and as the mourners in a broken row,
yet calm as monks, move down the turning track,
the new grave shouts from a black throat through the snow.

Disjointed relics in a blanket sack.
Cold, unstrung limbs. Dumb lips of a youth
who sang last night. He slapped the corporal's back,

the warming rum was pungent on his breath.
The Padre's prayers and our blunt orisons
sweeten to sickness the bitterness of death,

bring pathos gauche among the vulgar guns.
Given to cards. Fond of a naked swim.
Forget his name, an average of sons.

Oh, shovel the frozen clods of mud on him!
Make less fuss! Make haste, and let us go.
What if once his own and twisted stem

disturbed the soil, sprung leaves, was bold to grow,
to take up space and air between the sun and earth?
Look at the grave-stain in the crib of snow,

Look at our guilty thirty pieces' worth.

LETTER FROM MONTE STANCO

Mother, the weather is chill on these hills,
the soil is eroded, old;
there's a hint of blood on the ancient house,
on the leaves of the chestnuts' red and gold –
wherever the black track lurches, twists
up smothering heights to the cold;
as shadows we stalk in single file
with clobber and kit through drizzling rain
man by man, with weapon and will,
tackling the blasted hill again.

Pausing to shift the weight of my Bren
at the foot of the gravel steep
I watch in dusk the wounded brought down
slowly, by ambulance-jeep;
at the dressing station under the trees
those who're lucky, by twos, by threes,
will join the others who sleep, who sleep;
others who stalked in single file,
who tackled this blasted hill in vain,
wrapped in one blanket, stiff in the soil,
shut from the leaves, and the lead, and the rain.

Mother, I feel our single file
is doubled now in the dark;
this track is old, the mist's on the world,
and the hill is a question-mark;
shadows are men to the end of time
who can't care much if the end of the climb

46

is Golgotha's hill or the hill of the Ark;
a shadow with shadows I stalk alone
with timeless kit through eternal rain,
with the same one weapon, the human will,
mounting the heights of death and pain.

CHRISTMAS 1944. CASTIGLIONE DEI PEPOLI

The last field slips between the chestnut stems.
Far down below, the railway bridge's wreck,
black gunpits, transport random-parked,
thin files of soldiers on a contour track;
far up, beyond the woods, the summit's skull
seizing the sky with its ragged fangs of rock.

Raw is the rock, uncut by chisels; clean
trackless snow speaks no evangel.
The only movement in the earth and sky
is a silver fighter, splendid, single,
whose shadow, leaping the hillsides, hints
a sudden advent of death's angel.

A deep sea-silence presses on my ears;
sunlight, like a wind that beats the skin,
and clearer than my shadow on the snow,
harder than these ragged teeth of stone
in me lies faith a scattered skeleton,
Christ's cross burning, Bethlehem in ruin.

CAPE-COLOURED BATMAN

As the slanting sun drowsed lazily
on the terraced groves of Tuscany
at last I found him, back to a trunk:
Nelson, my batman, the bastard, drunk.

On the grass beneath an olive tree
his legs lay splayed in a khaki V
and all his body, relaxed, at ease,

head thrown back, while over his knees
strumming the banjo his yellow hands
stirred all his sorrow from four steel strands.

His melancholy cries from Hollywood,
'Where the coyotes cry' or 'Lady be good',
in that declining light awoke

a tenderness for the stupid bloke,
so happy his sorrow, so at ease
strumming the strings across his knees.

No doubt a pirate Javanese
from Malacca Straits or Sunda Seas
shaped those almond eyes of his;

a Negress from the Cameroons –
bought for brandy, sold for doubloons –
gave him a voice that wails and croons;

an eagle Arab trading far
from Hadramaut to Zanzibar
left him a nose like a scimitar;

a Bush-girl from the Namaqua sands
bequeathed him bird-like, restless hands
stirring his sorrow from four steel strands;

while English, Dutch and Portuguese
sick of biscuits and sodden cheese
put in at the Tavern of the Seas,

Northerners warm in the Southern night
drank red Cape brandy, and got tight –
and left him a skin that's almost white.

This is the man the Empires made
from lesser breeds, the child of Trade
left without hope in History's shade;

shouldered aside into any old place,
damned from birth by the great disgrace,
a touch of the tar-brush in his face.

Under pines, mimosas and mango trees
strewn through the world lie men like these:
drunk crooning voices, banjos on knees.

He fell asleep in a vinous mist,
star in his mouth, bottle in fist,
the desperate, maudlin hedonist.

But the pathos of the human race
sainted his drunken, relaxed face;
and a warm dusk wind through the olive trees
touched mute strings across his knees
with sorrows from the Seven Seas.

BITTER LITTLE BALLAD

When stale snow on the lower slope
lay thin and loose, a snake-shed skin;
when chestnut woods were soft with hope
and buds went juicy, white within;
when the smell of the sea stole over the land
our orders were signed by a neat, firm hand.

The waters of the melting snow
tinkled all night down moon-bright boulders;
impatient the primrose waited; and oh,
the peasant girl, hair to her shoulders,
clung to the soldier; hand in hand
they floated through a moon-drowned land.

From 'dromes far back four hundred kites
spun silver prop-coins into the sun.
Bombardiers itched at shining sights,
the soldier fondled his tommy-gun;
and everywhere grey trees shot green
defiance at death, and the skies were clean.

The sun threw shadows on the hills,
shadows of metal and mothers' sons.
The primrose split! A million wills
blossomed in bayonets, wounds, and guns.
With birdsong and Bren all over the land
Beauty and Death strolled hand in hand.

A shell burst in the small of his back:
a nasty job for the hygiene squad;
they wrapped the bits in a blanket sack,
the Padre muttered a little to God,
while, mocking his once so taut-strung spine,
lush tendrils reached from vine to vine.

As though that Spring could be undone
she shrank back into snow and mist.
Bitter against the golden sun,
she crushed the primrose in her fist.
Impotent, Summer shall depart
over the closed bud of her heart.

FROM A WAR DIARY: BEYOND VERONA

I am detailed to wait at the crossroads to give fresh orders
to B Company coming up. In clear warm sun I wait.

Drunk with wine and deliverance a man runs forward,
embraces me, kisses both my cheeks. I feel a bit of a fool;
but only a bit; nothing surprises any more.
'I'm South African! Free! Jeessuss Karyst!
East London! Buffalo River! Here I come! …'

50

I wait. Over the hedge a German boy so beautiful,
fair, with dead blue eyes stares at a bluer sky.
I wait, alive, technically alive, feeling
no gratitude, detached from passions shaking the world.

B Company comes up and gets its orders. I
look at my watch, then at my map. To make up time
I take a shortcut. A man leaps right into the road,
hands waving aloft, yelling like mad. I pull up.
He drags me by the wrist to the space before his door.
A growing crowd. We push through them. A youngish woman is
sprawling, keening, rocking to and fro
a young boy clutched in her arms. There's a small neat hole
in his forehead, his mouth hangs open, drools.
Her husband shouts at her, points at me. She lets
go of the child. It rolls to the dust. She rises, making for me,
all claws, and screaming. Her husband
steps between, shouts, explains. Women put arms around her,
she flings herself down by the boy.
They all start telling about it, over and over.

***

It seems their son had a bicycle, his dearest thing.
He was riding it round and round, look at these marks
fresh in mud, and shouting, 'Look at me, just look!'
Down this footpath here a soldier came running.
Sweating he was, and shaking. He wanted the bicycle.
The boy just clung to his dearest thing. He clung.
The soldier took his revolver out and shot him, dead.
He fired another shot at us, he grabbed the bike,
then, down that footpath there, he rode quickly away.

They knew that I could do nothing to catch the killer
nor give life to the killed. But someone had to be told.
They went on telling it over and over. Someone or other
had to be told. I listened, silent, over and over.
I had all the time in the world. When at last the father
picked up his son and went into the house I said
I'd report the matter, got into my jeep and rode away.

51

AFTER AN ATROCITY

I have nothing to beg dead Gods, no prayer
to utter this suffocating night,
not even a drowning gasp for air
a blind man's grasp at light,

not the frantic cry of a falling bird
above black floods for a rock or a tree
only a longing, pathetic, absurd,
for some other way to breathe and be,

an animal's dark insulted scream
from belly's pit, root of spine,
to scorch flesh free of this human dream,
to blast bones bare of the divine,

to be pure brute, utterly free
from such pretence, such insane pride,
to live in a sinless, wordless key
and have no need for the Crucified.

Ode

On first seeing Florence

ODE
On first seeing Florence

AUTHOR'S NOTE

There are in our existence spots of time
That with distinct pre-eminence maintain
A renovating virtue whence ... our minds
Are nourished and invisibly repaired;
A virtue, by which pleasure is enhanced,
That penetrates, enables us to mount
When high, more high, and lifts us up when fallen.
Wordsworth, The Prelude, Book XII.

This poem is an attempt to do justice to one such renovating spot of time. It was begun shortly after the experience from which it grew: an early-morning view of Florence before units of the 6th SA Armoured Division advanced to the southern bank of the Arno on 4 August 1944.

Although an early version of the poem won a poetry competition organised by the SABC in 1950, I was far from satisfied, and did not include it in my first volume of poems. I rewrote and expanded it in 1960, and again in 1964, when it was once more broadcast, to mark the twentieth anniversary of the liberation of Florence; but even then I knew that I had not done with it.

The disastrous Arno floods of November 1966 and a chance reading of Iris Origo's *War in the Val d'Orcia* made me return to the piece. As I now feel that it is as adequate a treatment of the experience as I shall manage, I have decided to print it, with thanks to those friends who, at various stages in its growth, have read and reacted to the piece; in particular, Charles Eglington, M R Cross, A G Woodward, Ruth Harnett and Sydney Clouts.

GUY BUTLER 1968

I

Earth shakes, spine jerks, eyes flicker to the flash
of heavy guns; tense as a dog's, ears strain
for the obliterating salvo's crash

upon our bivouac: but once again
it crumps far left. Dun gleam on tank and truck,
on dark tents taut from midnight's drenching rain

and dreaming towers deep in the campaign's muck.
And yet one dresses, dons unusual hopes
and steals abroad to try one's curious luck.

Far more than lungs are breathing as one gropes
towards the black hill's crest to catch a first
close view of Dante's town. Long, wooded slopes

secrete a blessed sense of getting lost
in scented labyrinths, until the lane
on one side falls away: sheer sky, where tossed

festoons of soft mauve cirrus sway between
the moon's dim burial and the unborn sun.
Transfixed, one stares. Why should the natural scene

seem to excel itself? Who dares poke fun
from such a stage? Lear's all-licensed fool
beneath this sky, after the storm is done,

might hold a tattered heart to ridicule.
Let tragedy alone; sit, smoke and take
a journalistic note. How soon through the cool

white-quilted mist will the hidden city break?
Behind my shoulders formal hosts of trees,
alert and breathless, guard a small cold lake:

dark pines, spear straight, in massive phalanxes;
loose-robed poplars, Parthian free and bright,
each poised to wheel and prance in the slightest breeze –

55

an old trick this, to take what comes to sight
from public day into one's private time,
fling words at it, then watch it catch alight

and, sparkling with live history, consume
its three-dimensional sheath of metaphor –
it's all in old Longinus *On the Sublime*.

Vanity of vanities – as though this war
should be fate's winnowing wind that sifts
the grain from all the chaff I've lived before.

One waits and smiles at one's own mental shifts.
Nun's fingers tell habitual beads to still
the heart for timeless prayer: so eyesight lifts

thing after thing, feels each, then lets it fall
till outer meets with inner mystery,
then pauses, holds it, and is held in thrall:

a pine is no mere non-deciduous tree;
each poplar celebrates its own white core:
once they were gods and oracles to me,

vast presences whose tall bone-houses bore
contrasting robes in whose deep shades I found
cool worlds to wander, dream in and explore;

but now oh how disturbingly they send
their minor chords vibrating through my brain
to where, half over earth's unending round,

their differing greens rise in a sun-blind plain
to splash damp shadows on the dazzling ground
about our house. Now I am there again.

II

There behind the shutters
at the moment when I found
the faces round the fire

unfocused, vague and strange;
when my attention wandered
from the familiar sound
of easy or eager voices
exploring the usual range
of politics and sport;
in their old-fashioned frames
the photographs of sculpture
had undergone a change;
they seemed to float apart
away from the papered walls,
leaving their pedestals
of rather self-conscious art:
glowing frozen flames,
they singed the ambient air
and scorched their guidebook names.
Rodin's ponderous Thinker;
headless high career
of that Winged Victory
out of Samothrace;
Delphic charioteer,
most balanced of all boys;
ball-of-right-foot poise
of Apollo Belvedere,
and Michelangelo's
tall David with lifted wrist,
slight frown and fearless stare
now waiting for me here
down in the quiet mist –
among whose solid forms,
Romantic, out of place,
a watercolour landscape
by old great-uncle John
in whom green fields and cloudforms
infallibly embrace
the artefact, the spire,
brick cottage, bridge of stone;
whose moist and breathing earth
has knowledge of no hours
but those which assure a man

that he is not alone.
This one was more ambitious –
no meadow sprigged with flowers,
but, loosely draped in woods,
smooth sides and breasts of hills
cascading down to distant
Florence and its towers.

Such daydreams might have geared
my adolescent will
to painting as career
had not the talk returned
to the Bible and such laws
as a man must needs fulfil.
Those faces had a look
which held the eyes: one learned
that trust in the Power of God
was living, still, and strong;
that the Pity of God the Son
still warmed, and lit, and burned.

III

The outer eye may notice how the mist
thins at the fringes, part of the mind may note
a tenseness in the diaphragm or wrist,

but such phenomena are quite remote
as moth or dogbark to the scholar who
on the eve of his greatest
find sat down and wrote:

I've done all I can;
there is nothing left to do
but wait. It's perfectly clear
who the chief agent is
and what the relevant factors are,
bar one, or possibly two.
One hopes, of course; but who
can force a catalysis?

The eye drifts over the mist, the pool, the trees,
and the mind drifts back to nostalgic analyses.

IV

One particular day,
rain-scented, when the breeze
was teasing the poplar catkins,
I blew inside and said:
A couple of thousand swallows
are back from overseas.
Mother stopped pouring the tea,
went to the window, stood
staring at the birds,
circling, scything the blue –
but whatever was the good?
Last month, it may be true,
they were over the Norfolk Broads,
the Serpentine, or even
slate-blue Crummock Water –
names, mere names to me –
but you never can tell with words.
My will took sharper aim:
someday, for sure I'd sever
whatever held me back
from my northern origins:
But why, already then,
did my guilty being shiver
as if on that black hillside
where the Devil almost wins,
where in a twilight cold
four women keen, imploring
a stone-deaf world to weep?
Was a hunger to see the world
one of the deadly sins ?

I wrapped my stripling flesh
in tapestries of gold
which shimmers with each movement,
glimmers, glows, or dims

as images flash out
or muffle in a fold:
a drowsy dragon guarding
ancient, dangerous gems,
or, surfing in on a shell
over the rustling green,
sun-touched, the blushing snow
of Anadyomene's limbs.

V

Mists move below; the rose-pink cirrus drifts,
but neither sun, nor towers in silhouette,
nor shell nor bomb-blast cracks the calm nor shifts
this eunuch's gloom which hankers a little yet
for antique shapes of passion or despair.
Tall forms that fall into my stare,
you're welcome to stir whatever Lazarus
lies wrapped in my limboed flesh: dark Tuscan pine,
and light-leafed poplar, glimmering nacreous,
come summon your shadows lost below the line.

In spring beneath a smooth blue skull of sky
from silver to green the poplar leaves would swirl
with a sound like the rush of rain, and a young boy's eye
would moisten with fearful wonder as at a girl.
But this Miss Greensleeves would go mandarin,
after a summer of deepening green,
in a loose kimono of gold; then stained-glass through
whose holiness red sun-blood streamed; then stark
fish skeletons white on the wintry blue
or nets for drifting star shoals after dark.

But neither December's throb nor numb nights of June
could shift the fine-spun chain-mail from the pine
nor make that northern stoic change his tune.
Over the poplar's passion to refine
the subtlest of responses to each season
he'd sigh his steady rhymes of reason,
his old heroic credo of restraint;

but in a young boy's heart the poplar could
scatter idolatry, a pagan saint
to all the restless peasants in his blood.

But every summer when the great heat blurs
most shapes and sounds, and a faint astringent scent
of the grey Karoo's drought-stunted heaths and myrrhs
gives mere survival its own sentiment
and keeps air calm though tortured by the sun,
the cones crack open, one by one,
the long-secluded shining seeds let go,
and give themselves to gravity, and spin
to slag-hot soils as graciously as though
life's only joy were spendthrift discipline.

Wing-shadowed by such trees I could forget,
deep in a distant book, the long dirt roads
naked of any legend, beasts unset
in shield or song; forget my people's loads
of loneliness, of unacknowledged needs,
long winds of exile blowing seeds
beyond the land's edge into the bitter sea;
upon a Persian carpet page I saw
tall Hector turn from pale Andromache,
the bronze, the blood, the black ships on the shore.

Oh, child I was, you favoured from the start
such legendary roads through deep word loam:
a banjo strummed behind a poultry cart –
you heard those great geese clamour over Rome,
Orpheus plucking death out of a string:
and with what easy zest you'd fling –
when red-earth dams were dry and skies accurst,
when prayers for rain arose from blackened farms –
your treble descant over the tenor thirst
for pastures green that quavered through the psalms!

But jabbed by a jackal bark behind your shoulder
as twilight sprung its trap on tent and flame;
seeing a cobra squirm, crushed by a boulder;

watching a black face wince – the knowledge came
of stark exposure and raggedness of heart
which neither nature, God nor art,
could hide or warm; then, sleepless, you might make
some slight acquaintance with your skeleton:
but never this bearable, this accustomed ache,
this waiting with little hope, or none, alone.

Dawn air contracts. Startled the poplars shimmer;
the pool glint dulls, and from their stirring tops
the pine-trees moan in sharps across the dimmer
wind's disturbance. Suddenly, it stops;
but over an inner pool dark leaves are shaking
an Eden where a boy is waking
to watch each hour's petal peal and float
slowly to earth; where close to the Tree that Knows
he wonders why the serpent's eye should gloat
over the day's disintegrating rose.

Child, unaware your universe was ending,
you still could be the thing you saw or heard;
had no vision of yourself, here, standing
sundered, hungry for miracles, and absurd;
though flanked, I'm dwarfed, by the same contrasting trees,
fiddling with ancient ironies,
the usual cluttered clichés of the Fall.
Don't hear the broken stutter of my throat.
No cliffs or lips would echo should you call.
Once they responded with a long, cool note.

VI

Earth shakes, shells crumping close! Quickly I fall
to feel the coarse earth shudder through my skin.
Pressing to it, prisoner to wall

I wait, breathless. When will our guns begin
their detonation, beat and blur, when, when?
One always knew one's chance was pretty thin.

A little different from one's dream of Man
this sweat-cold skin stretched taut on a skeleton,
the syncopated blood gone mad within,

battered from outside by the gun's dense din,
trembling, trembling. If a shell should pierce
this nerve-lit, brain-bright frontier between,

would anything survive the first,
the fierce embrace of darknesses? and this blind fright
be my last contact with the universe?

I force my eyelids open. Invading light
half-tames the outer sound. Quite odd that half
one's bestial fear should die at the kiss of sight,

this hazy jumble of sticks, grass blades and chaff.
The spine's high-pitched expectancy of death
relaxes with a shiver like a laugh

and in my throat flood great salt seas of breath.
The savage gun-bark flags. The grassy bars,
bent by my fingers, show an intact earth:

first one notes, deep-trenched with vertical scars,
a dark-stemmed pine; next, the pale blue bark
of poplar boles all stippled with sharp grey stars;

and then, beyond, out of the semi-dark
of Florence half-asleep, ascending straight
above dim window-flash and the Arno's arc,

steady as stakes in the mist's ebb-tide two great
stone towers! As different as these stems,
their colours, textures, shapes release a spate

of images in which each object swims:
the Trees! the Towers! designed and undesigned,
cut stone, scarred bark, refracted flowers and gems,

now separate, now closely intertwined,
float flaming in this legendary light
that inundates the valley and the mind:

resounding trumpet-clear into the white,
Arnolfo's tower elevates each pine
with its own granite into Yahveh's might,

a sundial of justice, human and divine;
Giotto's raises colours to the Son
in whom a thousand poplar trees combine

with hearts and minds that hunger to atone.
So Tower for tower, and Tree for tree you rise
above the last far salvo's fading drone

ringing and singing through space and time, through eyes
and skies, till in the first sun's level light
man, stone and tree stand stripped of all disguise

and seer and seen fuse in the arc of sight.

VII

A moment later one withdraws, amazed
at what this visionary landscape means:
like some young actor, introspective, crazed

by drilling in a bit-part that he scorns,
on whom one night, in some great scene he shares,
suddenly the play's horizon dawns:

the shriven stage has plateau space and air;
the tangled plot, his nugatory role,
are raised to passion, all is strict and clear;

then knows why his and every mortal soul
should move with joy, through every scene and act
as heirs to that compassion, that control;

so one relaxes, bows to the living fact,
plays with and into each responsive scene
to find dimensions which one thought one lacked.

VII

The mists have moved and other towers shine
one-sided to the sun; a mute, black bell
hangs clear within a belfry's arching stone,

while, scintillating, dawn's artesian well
filters a fountain freshness on the old
façades of palaces that stand as still

as those in tapestries long years have dulled,
except where fine-spun sunlight seems to stream
in tactile form off looms of water, gold

from Arno's weirs, until my own eyes seem
woven forever in the texture of this hour
woven forever in the substance of this dream,

shade of a tree, shadow of a tower.

IX

In oceanic stillness
I watch the great bell heave,
I hear a plummet plunging,
then wave by circling wave

from Santa Croce's bells
bells of the Carmine
spreads the fragmentation
of the living day;

as though on purgatory's
lower steps I lay
staring into heaven
through a lens of tears:

each tree and stone seems coral
ringed by a glittering play
of broken circles, echoes
from the singing spheres.

X

What tiny pulsing ball
of instinct, blood and feathers
flying ten thousand miles
after the flying sun
through shifting scenes and weathers
(long lakes of flashing glass,
savannahs green and dun,
leaf-like fanning veins
down which great rivers run,
siroccos, tropical rains,
silk skies and skies of brass)
through dewy morning haze
at last alighting nimbly
between a quartzite boulder
and tuft of winter grass,
ever stops to question
what directs its ways?

At moments such as this
one feels, as Hamlet did,
that neither lust enthroned
nor Machiavellian will
has power to make nonsense
of one sparrow's fall:
intellect and blood,
commingled well, respond,
with poise and grace accepting
the determined end:
the readiness is all.

XI

An echo dies; a continent disappears.
Indeed it seems as all the bells die down
that time is empty and the woven years

unravelled; the city is frozen in the sun,
as if the Arno curved around the Pole
and zero light for aeons glittered on

her silent weirs and streets without a soul.
It does not matter; like a bird I must
obey the swinging sun. The sculptor's tool

will break, remake till all we know is lost,
yet can't undo one day's existence, this
awareness in a sun-warmed scrap of dust

of all creation winging into bliss.

XII

Such moments leave one shaken
as if, by a Faustian trick,
one's eye had taken part in
a minor mystic's vision
and much less mediaeval
than romantic or baroque;
or by telepathy
with the absent-minded dead –
a stray electric thought
of a Shelley or a Blake,
or maybe Tintoretto,
had got into one's head
to break the bad old circuits
with its therapeutic shock.

Getting up and stretching
one slips into the normal
sense of time and being –
it's good to draw deep breath
like putting on one's nightgown
after the naked, formal
cool-blooded examination –
in which, while the mortal search
for trouble lasted, one felt,

much warmer than the doctor's,
the considerate hands of death.

Though I don't seek such moments
sometimes it seems to me
I spend the rest of my life
in silly circular flight
from their reality.
Yet back in normal dress
one feels, if not quite right,
at least not quite the freak.
Since Death cannot be banished
give him a good address
and an accent one can take;
since naked Life burns brilliant,
inhumanly so, let her
be dressed for decency's sake.

Old Yeats sings splendidly
that there's no consolation
for Man's embittered heart
but a breathless eternity
of intellect and art.
And Isabella talks,
and the old Duke wags at me:
Be absolute for death;
but I am in love with breath
even if I must walk
arm in arm with a tart
called Human History.

XIII

Yesterday a burial bell
between dull walls began to bleat.
Rebellious beneath its spell
I watched the cortège fill the street:
shrouded in red, dead partisan;
proud sullen faces, shuffling feet.

Those grim disciples have a plan:
no rite in some swept upper room
where God talks gently, Man to man:
the laws of love are null to them:
and hope is humbug here unless
the pay-off date's this side the tomb.

Who'll fill the one Word's empty space?
Eloquent abstract mysteries,
patterns of culture, class and race,
shall quell all private agonies
in mass crusades for shorter hours,
plus ampler goods and services.

XIV

And how long will you stand,
old superstitious towers,
against grey gales of words,
hysterical storms, and press
of multitudes whose fists
brandish scarlet flowers?

O white tree, tremulous,
let fall your leaves, be less
alive; turn suddenly
to stone, unshedding pine;
and all you varying bells
of joy and bitterness,
go dumb; for lost and gone
is joy's pure decantation
into personal song,
and the cry of the tongue as the heart
is frozen into stone.

XV

Comrade, cleanse your vision
of this mythical mirage.

To sing the red oasis?

Where young engineers
moisten arid soils
below a concrete verge
a landscape like Van Gogh's
near Arles or Nîmes appears.

My muse stays dumb.

Then listen
how gun-grey turbines whine
as once-wasted water-weight,
driving the armatures,
sends light to slumless suburbs:
see countless cities shine,
each with an acropolis!
Oh, use your brain; don't feel:
Beauty's born of use
and Justice of design!

To your clean Utopia
from this world torn by steel
one might set a gull-like sail
and saucily sheer apart
vast doldrums of the soul
with a cool polemic keel;
but I simply don't accept
your breezy little chart.

You're hopelessly addicted
to dead poets and their dreams.

My one concern is facts,
of history, and the heart.

Your mind still breathes the foetid
air of the catacombs.

In my small experience
evil is evil still

and hell has its full quota
of nice hygienic homes.

Your dialectic's anti-man.
Why should we still kneel
to a prophet man rejected,
scourged and crowned with thorns?

And what is your alternative?
A slide-rule or a wheel.
I nail my colours to a tree,
not to a slick machine.

XVI

The trees about me lift to a blue, deep sky
an architecture whose tall structure stills
all questioning: words, and wars, and wills
in these green cloisters make their peace and die.
Shriven, one lies and listens how one bird
rejoices in pure sunlight spilt and poured
into the brilliant pool; and then a calm
golden as that which crowned the seventh word
on that first Sabbath comes: the serpent's charm
has made as yet no pact with the absurd.

I stretch my spine, roll over, while a dear
remembered safety ripples through sense and limb,
then like a boy lie marvelling, aware
that bird and glittering leaf and stippled stem
and air too still to launch one thistledown
are part of me and quite as much my own
as their reflections and the brilliant blue
are part of the pool's so calm, so precious stone.
Mind seems a tender tensile surface through
which trees have thrust, skies dipped, and swallows flown.

The jewel cracks, the whole cathedral stirs,
clouds rush to martyr the sun. Afraid, alone
I watch wind's Lucifer; he breaks and blurs

each perfect image, sinks it like a stone
through splintered mirrors in whose darkest gaps
my own original darkness leaps and laps.
Hair-raising this, this sudden end, the sheer
sun-lit split-second when, being and ceasing to be,
my images break up, struggle, disappear
into the restless, unreliable sea.

No joy to me that each in an unquiet grave
shall undergo a dubious chemistry.
I have a dread of what the seventh wave
might lisp or thunder, sea-changed, back to me.
I've known an image step from its dead shell
onto the startled sand, so beautiful,
so unexpected that the poised mind, caught
off-balance, curses whatever powers send
such limbs to shatter the nervous light of thought,
to challenge its origin, to change its end.

XVII

Yet as I move returning,
wind rearing through the gaps
between dark copses, churning
smoky whorls of cloud,
last sporadic sunbursts
and, suddenly near, the first
loud thunderclaps –
so loud and close they bring
far Africa to mind,
making this landscape drop
its Tuscan mask, and be
simply the earth to me,
no other than it was
when at the age of six
near the foot of Alwyn Kop
its black outburst of noise
knocked me on to my knees –

I know that I am running
through more than normal weather:

scurrying, giddy leaf,
easily drifting feather,
grass-blades, water ripples
all crowding the selfsame way,
have something more to say
than the quarter of the wind.
I pause to listen better;
to glimpse through the coming storm's
gloom and jagged glitter
apocalyptic forms.

Footfall on the tympanum;
three faint but definite knocks
upon the flimsy back door
of the prophetic mind;
but none of my conscious keys
can pick the subliminal locks.

Yet though I am left to guess
whom I am not to meet,
the easy beat of my blood
tells me he comes to bless:
some king turned beggar whom
acquaintance with wind and storm
(frostbitten his sunburned skin)
has brought what a life of affairs
and battles never could:
Oedipus, close to Colonus:
Lear, lost on the open heath;
outcast, private souls,
so private they unsheathe
better far than the chorus,
fools, or philosophers can
the pitiless touch of greatness
in kings and naked wretches,
in universal man.
But since they cannot reach me
I guess what they might say:
The individual soul's
dark struggle to find its form

is more than his only means
to unriddle his origins
or tame a contentious storm;
in the last analysis,
be the end but a hint of the truth,
madness and blindness are bliss.

XVIII

Our tanks and trucks groan up the storm-tossed hill.
Through swirling skirts of raincloud, stunned, we see
All Florence naked, wet and shining, still.

Forever this wonder will inhabit me:
That mortal eyesight can embrace, transmute
Landscape and city, sky, tower, tree

To something so absolved, so absolute.

ELEGY
For a South African tank commander
killed in action in Italy, October 1944

A Sherman tank outside Chiusi

ELEGY

*For a South African tank commander killed in action in Italy,
October 1944*

Part One

I

Briefly released from autumn's battle line,
relaxed as antique shepherds on the sward,
or lounging like young lords, we'd savour wine,

we'd say the pen is mightier than the sword;
we'd nag at ironies: of how we'd come –
white Africans who artlessly abhorred

raw voices screaming from Berlin and Rome –
only to learn the bitter paradox
of trouble brewing, terribly, back home:

to help bring Freedom through the storms and shocks
to harbour in calm waters, victory won –
and then to run upon the selfsame rocks.

Talking universals large as the sun,
taking sweeping swaths of histories,
of Israel, Rome, Mohammed, Prester John,

we kept returning to those Portuguese,
daring the flat world's edge, whose light craft came
to pick the locks of all the southern seas.

Till then, to us, our land lay unknown, dumb:
we heard earth's rondure ring in Camoens's voice
and felt his proud foot pound the floors of time.

Who else could press such song from war and noise?
Into the epic vat what grapes he cast!
Sunburnt fidalgos, fair Grecian god-like boys

and princes gold as raisins from the East;
and so fermenting them till palates such as ours
still smack his pleasure in the troubled feast.

Great Europe, cradle of imperial powers,
far flung your boundaries of heart and mind,
we taste your sweetness, but the vintage sours.

We, from the outposts, meeting you half-blind
and lost among your ruins, we must call
on ancient, common ancestry to find

a voice to match our young worlds, walking tall –
and not the bitter, witty, weary strain
of greatness haunted by decline and fall.

II

Through days all raw with wounds and chilly rain,
dead sprawled in mud, blood blotching the green grass,
I hear a far bell tolling in my brain

lamenting still the death of Lycidas.
Its regal measure seems to ring and chime
from sunlit islands, pastoral, at peace;

its gentle pulsings of returning rhyme
delay the autumn in my exiled soul;
its mastery of seasons and of time,

transporting summer to the naked Pole
with quilts of green to warm the sleeping ice
does more, far more than comfort or console:

it vindicates the rites of speech and voice.
So shepherds, friends and poets worlds apart,
knowing that secret codes of sacrifice

are broken only in the listening heart,
in silence will escape, as if to kneel
before the blessed sacrament of art;

stopping their ears to earth's eternal brawl
they'll briefly slip into a timeless trance
before such beauty wrung from burial.

III

Long shadows lessen and the light dew dries.
The stolid pine trees fringe the mountain steep:
a classic landscape under azure skies

through which one shepherd and a dozen sheep
rustle dust-misty down the road. We stare
at them, at anything, to keep

our eyes turned off the pit: the stream's career
smooth-sliding through blue shades to where a cliff
breaks into white the sea's deep-green veneer.

If I were blessed with genuine belief
I'd cry to a Christian or a Pagan Muse
to touch my tongue, to single out this grief

among ten million others; let me choose
the proper vessel for men's tears, design
for all our angry anguish, and not lose

forever a friendship so much more than mine.
Familiar voices are abrupt and blunt.
Bite on the bullet, boy. No use to whine.

Art is a con-man with a clever stunt
of taking life's bedevilled pack in hand
to flash the happy sequences we want.

We ten will soon enough take up a stand,
obey a beautiful form of words, and prate
compliant with the worn-out church's grand

disguises and exposures of our state,
forgetting, in the ragged ritual,
how all his features will disintegrate;

like weathered statues on a temple wall
we'll form a well-spaced frieze. No private cries
must interrupt a soldier's funeral.

IV

The padre comes. See in his ice-blue eyes,
weary compassion; a black book in his fist;
and then four bearers tall, between whom lies

a weight so heavy that each inside wrist
is taut, a weight so dead each living arm
is stretched out stiff: a weight enough to twist

a little from the upright each tall form.
Bound in an army blanket, a mummy shape,
an outsize doll in a parcel, the human norm

roped neatly at the feet, the waist, the nape.
Nothing is here for tears, nor any sight
to raise the hairs of horror, breath of hope,

except that, dull and damp all down the right
side of his chest, his weeping blood has soaked
to glitter tell-tale in the curious light.

Yes, this is he. This carcass cursed and joked
in various lights of day, night, in between:
through driving rain trudged forward, heavy cloaked;

in no-man's-land, under a summer moon
he crammed his arms with silver-dusty hay
helping the peasants thrash their threatened corn;

last week his huge hands cupped a match away
from the sharp dawn wind to light your cigarette;
but what do these things mean, what do they say,

to us, or him? Spell out a pious debt?
Why are we here? To see what pole-axed fall
may be our own before three suns have set?

Choke back such questions. Preserve the sculptured wall:
be marble, hard within the mist and dark
that swirl across the place of burial.

V

We ten, who focus in a neat stone arc
the grave's hard lips and gag of ground, should bring
some human gesture to a scene so stark,

should be the armed retainers come to sing
the deep lament their hero's death demands.
but we, alas, are no such noble thing.

Though each knew him, bare seas and endless sands
divide our hearts, exiled and set adrift:
across these separate, ten, vibrating strands

no common plectrum dares to strike and lift
our sorrow to a single, plangent chord;
no, such a song would prove a Grecian gift

to hearts so Hectorless. Once struck, once heard
a common chord would stun the watching nerves,
and every heart, giving tumultuous word

to pent-up joy and largesse of our lives,
would rise to smash the stone, but saving, wall.
Far better each one separately grieves.

Beware of contact. Sing no hymn at all.
Forget the others. Be a single stake,
be driven deep to mark his burial.

VI

Let all lament be inward, let it not break
the stoic sky to sobbing, nor yet cause
a cypress or an olive tree to shake

or darker waves to stumble on these shores:
these quiet-watered shores whose surface now –
now while the bearers on the pit's edge pause –

shines brilliant green and tosses bough on bough
of lavish blossoms and dark, glittering leaves
towards the earth and air – still whispering how

foam-white Love slipped naked from the waves,
and how dim siren songs could fill the ear
to lure young sailors into craggy graves.

Oh, far and other the old godless roar
where Indian and Atlantic thrash the base
of sullen Africa: there red cliffs soar

to meet world-tides, world-winds, and bleakly face
the southern pole! Never the halcyon rocks
on those huge waters born of storm and ice …

Oh dear dear friend, that friendless ocean knocks
my heart. Although our poetry was born
by this nymph-haunted sea whose music locks

my mind still closer every dusk and dawn,
your death brings other airs to fill my mouth,
now cold as the winds that blast the plunging Horn,

now hot as the swamps and deserts to the south,
that deep to severing deep may suddenly call
and distance dwindle to the point of death.

The bearers step back from the blood-stained pall.
Flicking white pages to the proper place
the padre starts the rite of burial.

VII

Oh, linger at each word! Oh, make less haste –
once, as boys, while dawning mountains reared
their lamp-black paper-cuts against the east,

we rose, and cantered clear across the weird
scrub-stippled spaces while the frosty sky
was crackling with a sad and raucous bird.

Then for your happy head and dancing eye
what vast perspectives, what a skyline swung!
I see you still, loose, leaning recklessly

over the streaming mane. Slack the reins hung
beneath our horses' necks. Their pouring hooves
thundered dull in multiple rhythm, or rung,

sharp, for a second, on rock. A donga! Swerve?
No, risk it! Jump! O the loose, then taut
poise of your balancing body as you move,

centaur-knit to the long, then rapid, short,
folding and unfolding equine limbs!
Sky, wind, valley, all mastered in sheer sport,

you, life's pivot, to the grey horizon's rims!
Now, closer to the hills, we slackened pace.
Young heir-apparent, your practised vision skims

erosion, grazing, brak from place to place;
assessed the water in two red-earth dams
from which tromboning geese splashed up to trace

wide-echoing arcs of sky, while bronze-horned rams
faced round with stupid strength, and silver ewes
nervously nudged their crinkle-pelted lambs.

Reaching the hills, we let our horses choose
their sure footholds among the scattered rocks,
until at last, in waves, great sunlit views

broke on the eyes' foreshore. Forgotten tracks
dwindled below. In blue-grey spaces, slight
signatures of Man: white buildings, stacks,

dams, avenues. Yet your exploring sight
was not for these, but on their end, the edge
of dark hills cutting sharp against the light.

I saw the Trek in you, a tempered wedge
that cleft horizons open. Your shadow fell
far down the hill across the curving sedge.

Linger at every word. Oh, let me call
on that bare open height to see the sad
and viewless valley of your burial!

VIII

High ironstone hills and wide plateau who reared
his young blood to the sun, see where he lies
spilt in a little field the Romans cleared.

Born to the great escarpment's reckless size
he met a cramped and claustrophobic end.
Grey gunners mocked the sharpness of his eyes.

All camouflaged where leaves and stone walls blend
they waited, smoking, seeing but unseen,
with armour-piercing shells to hand. My friend,

in that late afternoon even the keen
crepuscular breeze deserted you. You fell
in coils of oil in the throes of a machine.

That cooped up death inside a tank's blind hull
conjures dark horror to attend us here
who stand, noon-bright, all round your burial.

Part Two

I

The arc we make is broken wide and bare
towards you, Africa! Alas, far south
the beams of love that should be focused here.

Although the rim of agony is all earth
and each death breaks a universal bread
the break is bitterest where the corn had birth.

Slowly he's lowered to his measured bed.
Soon he'll be sealed from this corrupting air,
from light that shows no mercy to the dead.

Why should I now remember, now, and here,
words said about our Africa by one
who took the world for his poetic share?

Camoens, imperial Renaissance man,
whose heroes, fetched from Troy, still strut and prance
from Lisbon and Malind: whose Grecian sun

takes Benin's Bight and Goa in one glance:
whose winds, though half-monsoon, half-Christian gale
swirl spice and candle-smoke in mingling dance:

above whose big-with-the-future, bellying sail
by turns Our Lady and lush Venus hover, –
how few your words for Africa, how frail!

In so much unknown, nothing to uncover
except one exiled god, whom rage deforms,
old Adamastor, the sea's rejected lover,

shaking his foaming beard on a Cape of Storms,
still blasting with the thunder of his curse
whatever Man in Africa performs.

Far up the Eastern Coast, struck by the terse
harsh sentences of death, your proud face winces:
all grandeur, suddenly, quits your regal verse;

furled are the flags, dumb are the drums of princes,
whole continents are drowned in depths of song
whose calm heroic irony convinces

bones lie best in lands where their hearts belong.
The passage I now remember, Camoens, tells
how many a scurvied corpse with rotting tongue,

you buried without requiem or bells
in unblessed ground upon an unmapped shore;
in mangrove shades, in grit of tropical shells,

abandoned those who staked and lost their share
on Fortune's wheel since leaving Portugal:
to save a hero's face from cruel air

use any passing wave or random hill,
as we did for these ordinary men.
there's nothing difficult in burial.

II

But do not stare, Camoens, at us ten
who hide a body on this alien shore.
Stare into Africa, beyond the line

of crags that echo Adamastor's roar:
look on a gabled homestead, white in the sun,
where a woman pauses in the open door.

She should be here. But nothing can be done.
We couldn't comfort her. You might have said
a simple prayer to Mary and her Son.

She moves across the yard, beyond the shed,
so small beneath the curving cliffs of sky,
to stand where trees across her other dead

throw shadows west and east diurnally.
Those lying there found Africa was good.
Where else should their extinguished bodies be

but in the soil that gave their daily bread?
Though Adamastor's curse seems strong enough
and our short history is dark with blood

this woman and these graves have power to prove
that exile ends where families hold still
and look on landscapes with familiar love.

But what use now the family graveyard's wall,
the marble headstones' lettering in lead?
Sad, futile pieties of burial.

III

And think: when she has read and once more read
the euphemisms in the telegram
her struggle to accept the fact: he's dead,

stone dead the weight once lively in her womb;
then, back like yesterday, the married spring
when she conceived him; then the joyful calm,

of waiting; back to the birth! And how she'd sing
him into sleep beside the poplar bush;
and later, laughed to see him leap and swing

on trailing willow withes, when summer's lush
and flaming leaves licked up against the grey
and wintry stems! Or when the evening hush

Enclosed the cooling house, and far away
slow cattle filed towards the round-stone kraals,
she'd lead him out to where his fathers lay

between dark cypress trees behind white walls –
the first to turn that soil, who'd fallen there
after far wandering as a wind-seed falls:

and tell him bitter things about their war:
how burning farms refined her people's faith,
a nation rising like the morning star –

was it for this she gave him limbs and breath?
A piece of flotsam in the imperial wake,
a foreign grave, an English priest at death?

Why did he leave her? Was the soil too weak,
the little orchard, the fields of maize? Too thin
the trekker blood? What drove him so to break

from their God-beaconed path? But deep within
she knows, like you, the old ancestral cause.
Could you refuse to bring horizons in,

to see strange mountains fall to stranger shores?
All earth is empty for man's heart to fill, –
how huge and empty now the homestead doors

as she returns, how empty and how still
the new-sown fields. Not all that stirring seed
will crack the sterile sheath off burial.

IV

Look, too, Camoens, on one who shares her need,
Yet will not touch her. Frowning and intent,
hiding a heart which few would guess could bleed,

his ageing Xhosa nurse-maid stands, head bent
unconsciously above her harbouring arms
where once his white resilience lay pent.

She bleeds for him, and for her sons, on farms
and far-off mines. Before he went to school
they all enjoyed the snow, the summer storms;

herded the calves; beside a shrinking pool
shaped yellow clays into a wide-horned team
of little oxen; rode on bales of wool

to railway sidings where the engines gleam.
But now she wonders, will his death break through
their hate or apathy, their stubborn dream

of cattle, land, instead of a goat or two?
A childhood memory of bright content
when skin meant nothing, cannot now renew

a wine gone sour in long years of want.
They'll merely nod, perhaps, and turn away
as if his death were quite irrelevant.

What utterance, what gesture knows the way
to scale or pierce the insulating wall?
Oh, there, as here, who has a word to say

that is not, like my own, equivocal?
The strangling cry of pity can't escape.
The noose is tightened by his burial.

V

So Black and White these tongueless women grope
across the world for dead or angry sons.
Darkness is closing on their days of hope.

Through blistered fingers the hot ash filters, runs.
Will all our country's motley various throng
be scattered so to sounds of sobs and guns?

I dread the triumph of endemic wrong
against which tenderness has no appeal.
These two stricken women must belong

among the universal host who kneel
about a Mother in whose aching arms
lies One our sins have pierced for burial.

VI

Far off two ageing men are talking of him,
then dumbstruck pause half down the civic stair,
lit soft, like Rembrandt's, in a downward gleam.

His absence meets his father everywhere:
still gibbing at all curbs on liberty.
impatient of tame titles 'son' and 'heir',

a proud young stallion haltered by the knee –
a family farm continues through the son –
'Now what do my thousands of morgen mean to me?'

From his horizon's rim a mountain's gone
and through that gap comes rolling a black storm –
white sheets of hail will pall this death at noon.

The other touches him gently on the arm.
He'd thought his brightest scholar born to bear
far greater sway than over any farm –

historian perhaps, or engineer:
he could reclothe dead things with living thought;
he'd see, beyond the concrete of a weir

the mind's creative barrier which brought
instinctive streams out of their ancient bed
to full canals, whose silvery fingers wrought

an emerald patch-work over arid red.
'What does it matter now? Our dreams are all
in vain.' 'But he is free.' 'He's dead, he's dead.'

Then they continue down, part in the hall,
and through the fractured sunlight of the street
are lost to the focus of this funeral.

Part Three

I

Dear friend, to whom our eyes revert again,
neat, trussed-up body by an abrupt pit,
we've told four mourners off like beads of pain

slipped from a thin-spun thread the fates have slit.
How little the ritual of this grieving means
to them, or you, insentient cause of it.

Whole avenues of mourners, indigo greens
of graveyard cypresses, the wild lament
of peasant girls, slow tears from kings and queens –

they'd only darken our predicament.
Your grave's an optic glass through which each sees
his own eclipse; the naked way we're sent

into confusions and uncertainties
without migration sense, without the sure
cyclical instinct of the changing trees.

Great as is the cause that brought us here –
what greater cause on earth than liberty? –
when death appears, abstractions disappear

and grammar crumbles when we come to die;
under the frown of individual grief
the finest phrases shrivel up and dry.

What arguments but love and deep belief
will ever revive the dying words we share?
Inheritors of Europe's falling leaf

each lonely will vibrates in icy air;
dead bodies do not germinate at all,
nor sprout, nor flower, in some other sphere;

and you'd not notice if I were to call
your name out loud, nor, falling by your side,
if my flesh meshed with yours in burial.

II

All features blur as bone and flesh divide.
Your classic profile, with the small birth-mark
on your left cheek, peels off, is putrefied.

This chestnut stem, in winter standing stark,
will profit from your awful entropy.
Your common salts, through roots and rings of bark

will bud and shoot into a song-filled tree;
your grinning skeleton below rejoice
at such outwittings of mortality;

your dead-weight lightened into rainbow days,
sun-, moon- and starlight through you rise and drift,
autumn shall strip you, springtime set ablaze –

alas, these gentling fallacies, the soft
and foggy answers to the question set:
what is their use? Are they the means to lift

our grief, put paid to friendship's untold debt?
We silent ten, like all compelled to face
interrogation by an open pit,

with unslaked throats will leave this bitter place
denied forgetful wine to mask the gall,
except the faithful priest, whose quiet grace

and steady voice define the ritual:
he knows the meaning of this sweat, this thirst,
these wounds, these tears: he sees through burial.

III

'Death, where is thy sting?' No defiant boast
supports this rhetoric. Gently, he,
in the names of Father, Son and Holy Ghost,

with raised hand signs a cross on the sky and sea;
and, at that sign, so simply made, the sight
of you, my friend, is given back to me:

a mass in a quiet field in early light,
and I, half envious, watching the ritual there;
seeing, surprised, how simple and contrite

you knelt on dew-wet grass in the chilly air,
and opened unpierced palms for bread and wine,
and took, and ate, your sacramental share.

Magnificent fable, that all our grief and sin
is known to One who shares in all our deeds,
whose hands are stretched to bless and bring us in!

Is it in vain the five-fold wounded bleeds?
Is death forever? My dear friend, are these,
are earth, decay, the gross sum of our deeds?

Is this the end of speech, or does a breeze
of questions part your startled lips? What fills
your heart, as, far below, our shifty seas

splash glinting with the sun's explosive shells?
Or do you journey purgatorial ways,
tried by the heat, refreshed at sacred wells,

until, at last, from some great height, you gaze
in careless wonder at the endless birth
of God's horizons in your answered eyes?

Spades grate, grit to steel. Clods of earth
thud on your flesh. Let all such questions be.
Soil smothers all. Conserve your spendthrift breath.

The shepherd who returns at dusk shall see
nothing remarkable except a small
irregular stain beside this chestnut tree.

Better not hope, best not guess at all.
Set down what ear has heard, what eye has seen,
the few and bitter facts of burial.

Part Four

I

It is finished. We pack up, pass between
the trees, enter our vehicles, revert
to cogs and levers of a grey machine

which smells of petrol, not of blood. The smart
of sunburnt arms, the jerk of the rotten road
draw all our suffering skinwards from the heart.

Discomfort comforts grief, and brings its load
of usual dumb tolerance. We move,
dull baggage mules beneath the war god's goad,

for miles. The fine dust gives each fist a glove.
Kilometers click between us. Inside
still swirls the slow salt sea of troubled love,

and lifts against the brain its little tide
obedient to an unknown moon. Heart cannot be
so simply silenced, simply satisfied,

heart has its own reasons, longs to see
sweet-savoured grasses bowed with heavy dew
and waxen candles of the chestnut tree

burn brightly in the glossy shade for you;
the primrose and small violet of the wood
yield every spring and summer ever new

garlands of grief to supplement the rude
outlandish wreaths our memories will weave,
in crowds, in queues, in bars, in solitude,

ever less often for your fading grave.
No sooner have I thought this than I feel
its falsity. Is there no way to grieve,

no act or art to catch and to recall?
Everything I say is but a sieve
which holds back only dregs of burial.

II

Worlds away from you our grey trucks leave
the main road leftwards, cross a stream, and stop.
We get out, smoke: some even wash and shave,

meet others, swop new rumours, talk old shop.
Cliché, swearword, gesture and set phrase,
are signposts on a semi-conscious map

which shepherd nervous thoughts down well-worn ways.
Questions? In clubs or favourite pubs few see
jungles or dying cities under the haze.

Draw up a chair and chat. There yet may be
a cypher to surrounding silences? None
except the dubious gods possess the key.

So shuffle the pack of words. It's time you won.
You'll find you have some aces. None at all.
The pack's been stacked since human life began.

Take up the casual sequences as they fall.
Some think the world makes sense, while others say
a game of chance which ends in burial.

III

Exhausted by this all-too final day
I lie upon my back, and smoke. Distress
Has gone. The heart is quiet: but, still at play,

the mind keeps asking: is this meaningless?
A dozen coloured batmen, drunk, alive,
start riding with a ribald recklessness

upon a banjo's back. Their songs revive
more than a mere nostalgic Boland scene.
It's true they sing like this at home to thieve

a hot ironical night of joy between
the rancid drudgery and the reckless dream;
but here, tonight, their sharp electric tune

explores the dusk with shifty, flashy gleam,
and on the dumb, in drunkenness or death,
plays an hilarious and irreverent beam.

Now, rising to dance, they trample underneath
all other sounds except their song's mad rhythm,
then skate upon the ice their bacchic breath

has crystallised across the boiling chasm.
But when they stop, watch, watch the surface crack,
the dance dismembered drown in twitch and spasm!

Cannot the old organic age come back
when through all dance and ritual song there burned
pervasive warmth which our new systems lack,

a sun round which both death and life once turned
with neither dark nor light the end of all?
Pursuit of light alone is all I've learned;

blindness to death has made life trivial;
for what's the worth of cosmic words and maps
if we can't gloss or place one burial?

IV

Slowly I stroll the silent, twilit slopes
and long for the animal earth-bond to return.
Nothing but distances. My being gropes

at blind-man's-buff among the hills. The fern
is simply fibre, rough in my hard clutch.
Oh, I know Narcissus must die, or learn

that Nature's pools and woods can't give him much
but self-reflections: she has no reply
except to echo. Only the thunder's touch

which shivers the glass, only the sudden cry
of creatures cracked by pain or bliss, can give
weight to his words and vision to his eye.

But this goes deeper far: how can we love
when every outward gesture, thought or word
must see itself distorted, relative

and mirrored in the infinite absurd?
If speech is but a subtle sort of bark,
and song the pretty twitter of a bird,

why should it hurt to hear a falling lark
stutter so sweetly? Why do I choke and turn
to mutter half-meant longings to the dark?

I would you slept where grey mimosas churn
cream-yellow pollen on the tombs, and tall
red aloes, winter's candelabras, burn

on all the hills: where, once the spring rains fall,
the silken freesia from its silver stalk
might swing a censer for your burial.

V

My dear dead friend, what causes me to talk
this broken dialect of grief, to bring
Time's withered garlands as I weep and walk?

94

Why can't I make a song of suffering,
give you a resurrection? Oh, to place
you among our stars – not these first, glimmering

rush lights in a darkness damp with loss –
but in the brilliant scatter of our sky,
the sharpest shiner in the Southern Cross,

from which you could look down perpetually
on plain, and hill, and sea! But I must leave
these thread-bare classic fables, must, since we

have stripped the stars of myth and cannot grieve
in patterns of such loveliness. All, all
my pathless heart can do for you is weave

its own confusion round your little fall.
No spell survives to weave a deathless star
into the fabric of your funeral.

VI

No resurrection. Now you'll be no more
than some small fragment of a song one hears
struck from the heart's erratic old guitar

in noisy suburbs of collapsing years:
a sentimental chord, grown almost trite,
mixed up with offered smokes and ordered beers.

Yes, it has to happen. Although I fight
against this vision of your second death
by scurvy in our minds, this lovely night

that pours upon the trees, the rocks, the heath,
is the first diseasing wave, a mouldering
of images within our minds' warm earth.

How small our world is, small! How weak a thing
our flesh! Above the dead Renaissance dream
great lines of guns and air-fleets roar and ring:

in Africa blind lightnings crack and gleam
down towering clouds; rock strata lose their grip;
there's blood not water in each dam and stream.

And I have failed, am lost, must blindly grope
through slums and deserts of my heart, and fall
into the shame of impossible hope;

drowning in myself, must cry and call
across the seas and continents and skies
for One who walks the waves of burial.

Europe and South Africa
1945–1954

Les Baux

STRANGER TO EUROPE

Stranger to Europe, waiting release,
my heart a torn-up, drying root
I breathed the rain of an Irish peace
that afternoon when a bird or a tree,
long known as an exiled name, could cease
as such, take wing and trembling shoot
green light and shade through the heart of me.

Near a knotty hedge we had stopped.
'This is an aspen.' 'Tell me more.'
Customary veils and masks had dropped.
Each looked at the hidden other in each.
Sure, we who could never kiss had leapt
to living conclusions long before
golden chestnut or copper beech.

So, as the wind drove sapless leaves
into the bonfire of the sun,
as thunderclouds made giant graves
of the black, bare hills of Kerry,
in a swirl of shadow, words, one by one
fell on the stubble and the sheaves;
'Wild dogrose this; this, hawthorn berry.'

But there was something more you meant,
as if the trees and clouds had grown
into a timeless flame that burnt
all worlds of words and left them dust
through stubble and sedge by the late wind blown:
a love not born and not to be learnt
but given and taken, an ultimate trust.

Now, between my restless eyes
and the scribbled wisdom of the ages
black hills meet moving skies
and through rough hedges a late wind blows;
and in my palm through all the rages
of lust and love now, always, lie
brown hawthorn berry, red dog-rose.

FAREWELL IN A FORMAL GARDEN

This, I suppose
is much like any other
November day beside the Thames:
damp, blue gravel, a blackened rose,
and the farther trees in the fog's thick smother
invisible but for their wind-torn hems.

The hedges of box
as dark as ever:
the eye, pursuing their parallel run
halts at the solid paws and locks
of two bronze lions that roar for the sun
from the brink of the tamed, indefinite river.

The hard beside
the soft,
objects in the mist's alembic seem
unidentified,
losing identity, already lost
or suddenly clear and sharp as a scream.

My love, so we
at this particular year's
normal, inevitable dying,
dissolve in mists, fade, cease to be,
only to meet these nerve-trees frosted with tears
and hail-hard words across the breeze of sighing.

AUBADE

Disintegrating, the coals split, crack
in the grate, shedding a dying heat.
The mantle clock
shall soon despatch on jack-boot feet
indifferent thugs to force me back,

fling you aside and snap the lock.
And there's nothing, nothing we can do.
All fires die, all nights must end
in desired dawns
or unwanted days: and the loves of two
like insects left on the yellowing lawns
die in the weathers that freeze and rend.

Look through the curtains. Our lover's moon
has lost her broken ring in the mist.
Each lamp's a nightmare place,
a wet tar-stage where limp leaves twist
in sad little ballets devoid of grace
to scraping winds that know no tune.

Soon shall the burning in our limbs
be ash and acrid smoke, arms stripped
of this green tenderness;
heart shall be naked, zero-gripped,
birdless, black; its living dress
lie stiff in cold, stopped streams.

No hope of meeting? Spring together?
None, none. This dawn shall damn each heart
to different stations,
to different cities seas apart,
days, weeks, years, in opposites of weather.
Cold stars, great gales divide our destinations.

Though now, in spite of Time's blind rush,
sad limbs still burn exquisitely,
our quay-side kiss
shall strangle, shall drown in the open sea.
We tremble in the bubble of our bliss.
Never was horror like this hush.

A DREAM AFTER VISITING STONEHENGE

                              ... A wind
arose which, moving with an equal pace,

felt through the veins and creases of each mind
combining countless whispers into one
legato chorus of the unresigned

deep envy all flesh cherishes for stone.
The sound rose up and seemed to spin and sway
against the crater's curved and mouldering cone

about whose base, scree-brittle leaves, we lay
immune from spring's resurgence in the root
but cut from the quietus of decay.

We heard our longings in that wind's deep flute:
'O megaliths grey in the moonlight, caring and knowing
nothing of pain in plant or man or brute

or what lost hopes this quiet wind is sowing
through your great cirques and avenues of stone;
eroded rock, untouched by death or growing

accept us, petrify, make us your own!
End the dark heart's unintended treasons,
its blood miasmas, harrowings of bone,

and cold deliriums of crystallising reasons;
teach us merely to be, to roll and turn
through stellar rituals and sapless seasons,

off the orbit of hope, safe from the burn
of flower, sun, or the sudden flame of a girl;
and more, far more than all, never to mourn

for the lost ridiculous chance to buy that pearl
whose pure enduring rondure mocks mere stone
and in whose heart whole universes whirl.'

LETTER TO DESMOND AND NORAH STUTCHBURY, JUNE 1946

Seven hours flying over empty sea and sand
shook nerve and brain to their nadir. Even the not
quite unexpected Nile (a copper-hot
cobra asleep on the Delta) seemed ordinary, and,

naturally, always there. But now, now its Almaza,
a grass chair, cool beer, a lawn, and a ragged palm.
And peace. Peace, till the torrid continuous calm
gnaws at my slavish self, as it did one eyeless in Gaza.

Shall I smell out a Delilah? Blame these eyes put out
on scapegoat Philistines? No. No, I was blinded
to any moments that mattered by being bloody-minded,
by making a point of honour to call this earth in doubt.

I'd watched my few remaining heroes submit to being ground
by habit, routine, ritual; seen them return to normal,
escaping the vision's ache by being strictly formal;
I saw the great occasion pass, and no faith found.

Or back at college or office, seaside or swimming-bath,
as scars grow faint, so over the flame they draw
the same old safety-curtain, Bourbons about the war.
But why the hell should I talk? I fell for 'the aftermath',

sulking long months in England: 'The game's not worth the
                                                    candle.
Touch has deserted our fingers; a query haloes each head;
life is a termites' nest under a pervert's sandal,
and the heroes, O the heroes, are irredeemably dead'.

But here, in a mental and physical sweat,
in transit between two hemispheres,
weary of wangling stocks and shares
to Better-forgotten from Don't-forget,

I switch off thought, relax in my chair
and sink to a tingling, sensual daze:
I burn where giant flamboyants blaze
scarlet into the sunset air.

Thus for one moment, till I close
my lids; then, back in your twilit room,
I listen to last week's talk of doom:
how I mourned in the scent of a crumbling rose!

But you did not, nor did you think
Europe's end would be 'death and madness',
were short with singers of infinite sadness
whose robes are purple and black untouched by gold or pink.

Laughing aloud at luxurious Grief
weeping her maudlin Virgilian tear,
you brought me the birth of another year,
awoke a wish in me to return to myself, and live;

And as you spoke I heard the green surf
of spring over England break outside; the surge, the lap
on the darkening lawn, the blossom, the sap
surely asserting itself in stems and the heavy turf ...

Remote above Mecca the aqueous air
crystallises out into stars that could cut the hand.
Little remains to be said. This moment, in every land
the world is one for the watcher; this moment, I

am one with the two of you, dark and blonde,
who once, pressed back by bayonets and iron
stared over the sea to rising Orion,
and heard your hearts beat loud beyond.

HOMECOMING

Hearing noon-bells chime
under my boyhood sky
I knew my heart had become
a metronomic drum:
mere continual time,
not moments, passed me by.

Not the larger stature of the trees
nor the new road ruining the quiet hillside
had muddled my clocks and maps;
but the heart itself, fogged with lies,
afraid of being crucified
on hills where clouds collapse.

Yes, this is still the same dear place,
the identical sun that shone;
it's only the courage for the quest
and the relish for heights has gone.
The open hand is a fist.
Fear has hardened the face.

The street was once a bridle path
where singing I strolled alone.
Mute on the kerb, mere aftermath
and wreck of a braver me,
I smart as the workmen fell the tree –
green ruin on disciplined stone.

REMEMBERING 1939

Withdrawn, high in the hilly grass he lay
nailed by his longing, in the lazy sundown's
solitude. Winds lapped round the empty bay
of the sky, its depths stirred through the town's
grey coral reef. Troops were already parading

104

in the arclit market square. Verbs and nouns
exploding in headlines, loves and hates invading
his cool and neutral heart, still sentryless, still bare
to the stab of a kiss or the slow, degrading
exposure of soul to everybody's stare.

The westward drift of half a dozen birds
across a strand of cirrus struck a sudden chill,
made him aware, beneath his anxious will,
that a sudden shift in images was near,
a deep conspiracy below the map of words.

Headlines and radios were crying Come!
And though at length he left the quiet hill
to enter the human city with its dumb
cry for meaning in the heart of all its noise,
part of him stayed put, would never budge.

Never quite knowing why
swigging his rationed brandy, swopping smut with the boys,
flirting in cabarets, addressing letters home,
suddenly he cut quite loose
from the crazy-mixed-up music, the sloppy or lethal words,

and sure as a migrating bird
over the junkyards of hatred, the jungles of love,
heartless, complete for the moment, would move
to feel and hear the inhuman breeze stir dry
the seeded grass above the city's smudge.

AFTER TEN YEARS

Once, from this hill, I saw beyond the city,
beyond exploding headlines, the great Republic
of men all stalwart, straight as pines in the sun.

Now, no vision: a glittering hurtle of hail
in hard diagonal shafts from thunder-clouds,
and night coming down like a curse on the city.

105

The dream, the dream, dies hard, dies now in this
uncharitable dusk. Like love, it leaves an aching
uselessness. If only the empty eye

Could anywhere find an altar, in the city,
beyond, or in the storm: if only to cry:
'I have hope: we shall master our dream!'

Walking back through the wet it would be easy
to sink my voice in a mass concord, or plunge
down death-wish dreams to Götterdämmerung.

***

Midnight, with no bells, no ghosts, no meaning
starless midnight, measureless, oppressing
from pointless Space the small, proud arclight, Mind:

the arclight beating down and inward, down
on the tense arena of appetites and nerves:
risk of the agile reason, rush of the bellowing passion,

round the clock and the months and all four seasons
the same, same game, whose crowd cannot disperse,
not even on Sundays, cannot look out or up

through a steep ascending gothic nave or over
a curving recession of hills: for the common sky
has banished the royal sun, and the level world

that butts on their backs has neither a work nor a worship
to claim the whole strong heart of a normal man.
Where is the outward turning, the large embrace?

The taste of rain? The ritual act of faith
lifting the actor out of himself, and touching
terrestrial things with a glimmer, a guess at God?

Must we reply forever: 'How shall we see,
apart from the arclight? None masters the night except
simpletons, kids, and saints who carry a candle,

a faith no sensible man can ever believe in.
Let's stick to the things we know, continue to make
our daily mass on dust and adrenalin.'

***

The storm stops thrashing the unlit window.
The whimpering winds go to earth in the woods.
I open the sash, I search for the calm outside.

Sky cloudless, almost starless; at peace, serene,
harbouring a moon whose sodium light
pours over city and world a molten mould.

So simple the system of planets, the dance of the earth
and the moon: so simple, predictable, sure
the sequence from summer to winter solstice

that I, who once held men would rise and throng
like equinoctial seas concerted to the moon,
would weep, if there were use or strength in tears.

The freeze begins. From lintel and from sill
up and down, blue, hard, the icicles advance
till they meet in my spine and pierce my tongue:

and still I stare, still stare with empty eyes
at the moon, and the shadows of trees, flues, walls,
and telephone poles obeying her shakeless beam.

***

After the negative night, the voiceless vigil
through rigid groves, up frost-paved paths I climb,
obedient still to the once miraculous hill.

About me trees, animals await the sun.
For them spring is sure, is approaching now
a limit to leaflessness, long nights, cold;

but for us there is no inevitable ebb and flow,
no guaranteed end to twilight or night, no
springtide migration in search of the sun;

Instead, arrested dusk, autumnal time,
fermenting fruits, a troubled and sulky season.
The corn gods are dead or dying. Folk no longer

live for a resurrection, no longer look
to rebirth of Man or of God, no longer hope
for the anger of spring or the summer fever

sweeping a nation, a city, or even a town:
the lens of the whole world's light and warmth,
the candle and hearth of the heart is dead.

Instead of devils and gods, neurotic shivers
at private assassins an inch below the skin.
O sharp death-ache descending on the lovers

who wander down huge canyons flanked by flats,
wondering, looking up, seeing no stars at all
but light-crazed moths round numbered standard lamps.

Naked the forest straggles through the wintry light.
Far, beyond the frost-furred basalt, fret
the heavy, never-folded forepaws of the sea.

Dim cities smoke and stir between: but here
level the sun strikes first, strikes clear and candid
into my face and eyes, my cold but unclutched hands.

I accept my pain. I am incomplete,
cannot measure, build or synthesise;
I lack a means of dimension, a corner stone,

an essential catalyst. O hidden God,
sweet Giver of faith, still veiled, unknown to me,
humbly I start again, set out to rediscover

you with uncensored senses: shedding all dreams,
departing all cities of words, I shall wander
curious as a child, vulnerable as a lover:

let dawn your Son in joy, or pain, or wonder
in anger or kisses on these open pulses.

108

MYTHS

Alone one noon on a sheet of igneous rock
I smashed a five-foot cobra's head to pulp;
then, lifting its cool still-squirming gold
in my sweating ten separate fingers, suddenly
tall aloes were also standing there,
lichens were mat-red patches on glinting boulders,
clouds erupted white on the mountains' edge,
all, all insisting on being seen.
Familiar, and terribly strange, I felt the sun
gauntlet my arms and cloak my growing shoulders.

Never quite the same again
poplar, oak or pine, no, none
of the multifarious shapes and scents that breed
about the homestead, below the dam, along the canal,
or any place where a European,
making the most of a fistful of water, splits
the brown and grey with wedges of daring green –
known as invaders now, alien,
like the sounds on my tongue, the pink on my skin;
and, like my heroes, Jason, David, Robin Hood,
leaving tentative footprints on the sand between
the aloe and the rock, uncertain if this
were part of their proper destiny. Reading
Keats's *Lamia* and *Saint Agnes' Eve*
beneath a giant pear tree buzzing with bloom
I glanced at the galvanised windmill turning
its iron sunflower under the white-hot sky
and wondered if a Grecian or Medieval dream
could ever strike root away from our wedges of green,
could ever belong down there
where the level sheen on new lucerne stops short:
where aloes and thorns thrust roughly out
of the slate-blue shales and purple dolerite.

Yet sometimes the ghosts that books had put in my brain
would slip from their hiding behind my eyes
to take on flesh, the sometimes curious flesh
of an African incarnation.

One winter dusk when the livid snow
on Swaershoek Pass went dull, and the grey
ashbushes grew dim in smudges of smoke,
I stopped at the outspan place to watch,
intenser as the purple shades drew down,
a little fire leaping near a wagon,
sending its acrid smoke into the homeless night.
Patient as despair, eyes closed, ugly,
the woman stretched small hands towards the flames;
but the man, back to an indigo boulder,
face thrown up to the sky, was striking
rivers of sorrow into the arid darkness
from the throat of a battered, cheap guitar.
It seemed that in an empty hell
of darkness, cold and hunger, I had stumbled on
Eurydice, ragged, deaf forever,
Orpheus playing to beasts that would or could not hear,
both eternally lost to news or rumours of spring.

TO A STATUE OF THE VIRGIN
Seen near Les Baux, Provence, July 1947

I

Girl of stone, too white against this dark
catastrophe of cypresses, too cool
between sun-angry rocks and heat-split bark,
who ever placed you here? Your pedestal
is far from the huts: the wind frets, and the lark
falls pell-mell down to acres dry and small.

Who set you here with shy eyes, who made fall
your moulded arms in folds of too-dense vesture
so heavily, submissively, that all
sorrow and joy are wanting in your gesture?
You have forgotten the bitter Syrian pasture,
the ox, the ass, the crude, sharp-smelling stall.

110

Your body's virginal contour barely presses
against the nunnish robe, so cold it kills;
your lips' Magnificat no more confesses
to slaking a midday thirst at these thin rills;
O swathed in visions and songs above our distresses
you never were native to these niggardly hills!

And yet, for all the charm of your baroque stance
a slight ill-balance, a hint of hesitation
withholds you from the abstract, heavenly dance,
as if you heard a cry of consternation
and paused, but dared not turn your eyes to glance
into this pit of boredom and sensation.

Surely I see a likeness to lost Eve
haunting the woman in your face, contending
vainly with its blind-eyed peace. O leave
this bloodless bliss, this meekness and this bending,
return to our touch! Smile, weep, grieve,
O once-warm home of the Dove's descending!

II

Remember, Mary, that enormous noon,
Queen of heaven remember
the village girl you were:
simple, ignorant
that shepherds and kings from near and far
in less than a year would jettison
their crowns and crooks to kneel
to your sane pure message of mercy,
O dew on the basalt book of law.
Having made the beds and swept the rooms
you washed the dust from your hands with earth-cool water
and, with a glance through the small window
at the quivering, towering blue
shook the cares of the world from your mind
never remotely guessing
that even dying Narcissus across the Aegean
surprised by a voice far sweeter than Echo's would raise

111

dark startled eyes from the steel imprisoning brook
escaping himself at last in ripple on ripple of praise;
then went out, into the garden,
and, choosing a spot in the shade,
head leaning against a weathered wall,
composed yourself to prayer
quite unaware
what thunderheads with scented moisture stored
shadowed old Sinai and all the desert of laws,
or what calm tides brimmed Rome's long shores,
what fresh winds were hovering
on the fringes of the world.
Sun, hill, shadow,
far shepherd's monotonous flute
were simply there and themselves, yet all
love-things of God, like your body:
one hand wrapped like a marble frond
the other an opening almond shoot
lay limp in your lap together

but in that barely breathing calm
will and heart, unfussed, were busy still
sweeping, garnishing,
preparing for the presence
of Israel's Lord.

Then the olive that shaded your head
laden with setting fruit
in a gust from nowhere whispered, swayed
itself and its shadow a second
then stilled its every leaf
and was mute.
The far flute hushed
even the solemn bee
that hummed in the court all morning
went suddenly dumb.

The shimmering angel!
You had not seen him come
but there he was, celestial knee

splaying the soft grass, brilliant head
between your eyes and the mat-green leaves.

Then the first Hail Mary struck at your heart.

What could he mean?
On your choice hangs
the second creation of the world.
The noon sun sending
its shafts like hail
upon you, begs
to orbit between
your trembling hands.
You slipped to your knees,
your forearms crossing below your throat,
neck bent forward, blind.
Behold the handmaid of the Lord.
Then hands fell wide and open,
spine straightened, eyes lifted,
and you smiled:
Be it to me according to Thy Word.

Accepting lips had opened, never to close.
All space, all time, heaven, hell, were dumb.
The restless bee drank deep in the open rose.

III

But we are men for whom
All miracles are dead.
Our dry days drag and wander
to various silly deaths.
Blasé, or catching our breaths,
we pose, or fidget, or ponder
before a padded tomb.

Girl, give us what we need:
bring taste back to our bread,
revive the country dance,
bless the barren bed.

Kindle, if only once
such love of heaven and earth
that we may get a glimpse
of the glorious star above
that sordid stable birth.

Girl, give us what we need:
no, not Time at all
nor all Eternity,
but simply one split-second,
outside, beyond the Fall:
one static moment, freed
from the drum-beat of the sea:
a pause between two pulses,
a moment unlit by the sun
where nothing has ever been done
or ever been left undone:

Where the mist-blind ship and the rocks,
the back and the brine-dipped rod,
the quarrel of cube and dome
and the love and the wrath of God
are purged of paradox:
where all our prodigal meanings
returning, are welcomed home.

We know we lack you, Love.
Hands fumble for a gift.
Our hearts' long empty trees
stretch skyward for the Dove.

Sweet Maid, lift up your arms,
let lip and limb accept!
Rose of the earth, burst now!

The cyclone drift is still,
since noon all sounds have slept.
Empty of breath or bird
air that your own Son breathed,
earth on which he slept,

still wait, O Mary, wait,
still wait upon the Word!

IV

Then she said:
not in the written word
nor the terrible tears once shed
will any find
the Eternal Mind,
nor in a voice long dead.

None shall gather
the Will of the Father
thinking of Yea and Nay.
O so she said
beginning to keen and sway
looking down on her Dead.

Some may discover
the heavenly Lover
between the stabs and the caresses.
O so she said
unbinding her heavy tresses
bowing her beautiful head.

Some stumble on
my only Son
between the heart and the sword.
So she said
weeping above the silenced Word:
not by eyes is the message read.

Then she said
cradling again the murdered Word,
breasts pierced by His thorn-crowned head:
be still as stone.
Must God alone
know what it means to be dead?

TO AN ARTIST FRIEND: FLORENCE 1947

Dear Corduroy,
I saw today
the Massacios in the Carmine,
and really have nothing at all to add
to what you said: 'They're not so bad.'
But it wasn't the late, inadequate light
which mitigated my delight
but something which, I admit from the start,
is right outside the realm of ART:
in short, I must admit to be
influenced by Geography:
climate, flora, fauna, such,
matter, artistically, much:
the arts of different continents, thus,
should not be homogeneous.

While dozing in the Hotel Roma
a vivid flashback lit my coma, –
pictures which gave me as a boy
a quite unmitigated joy:
I'd climbed to the cave: there, on the rock
dim palimpsests of beast and buck,
moving motionless, for all to see
through century after century
in generous variety:
a living world, and left for us
by a primitive artist, anonymous.

This came at a time, I should suppose
when I was aware of aloe and rose –
of what had crossed the seas with us,
and what belonged – indigenous.
The Botticelli on the wall
old tales, old poetry, brought all
far Europe into imagination –
and emphasised our transplantation,
e.g. the Christmas cards that came
made me wince with quiet shame:
a robin-redbreast all aglow

on a cottage window thick with snow
sent from scorching Upington,
a hundred and sixty in the sun!
Had no one either eyes or ears
for the differing clocks of the hemispheres?
As if we lived in a hired house,
not here for good! Ridiculous!

But it's taken this Italian day
plus frescos in the Carmine
(and a coma
in the Roma)
to make the issue obvious
to me – and, dare I hope, to us?

We share, thanks be to ancestry,
Bruegel, Giotto, the whole Uffizi:
but, I contend, African light
calls from a different kind of sight.
We all respond to imaginative
brilliant shocks from the primitive,
simple, space-sure drawings that state
how excellent and accurate
were eyes trained by our air and sun
before White Africa began.

African objects have to face
terrific pressures of light and space.
Aren't you tired of aloes which seem
strayed out of a mystic Irish dream?
Sick of studies of native faces
empty of all human traces?
Of placid paintings of the Reef
without a hint of gold or grief?
As if in a brand-new continent
our art is already decadent,
and courage, insight, fury, fuss
were censored or superfluous!

Humbly, therefore, I propose
to wed the aloe and the rose,
but lest it prove an awkward match

117

(like corrugated iron and thatch)
I beg each would-be genius
to ponder my proposal – thus:

Give yourself to Africa!
Be proud, and boast, be jealous of her:
for she will not unveil, reveal
an ear or eyelash unless you feel:
nor will she share her secret state
with smugness, indifference or hate.
Sit with paint-stained hands to your chin,
stare long at her, learn discipline,
yield and suffer until you find
her splendour dancing in your mind,
violent, lovely, frivolous.
Do this, or miss the creative bus.

Next, if you wish to understand
the subtler gestures of her hand
find out just what you feel and mean –
you, her lover – by 'European'.
Go, get to that tiny continent,
source of eighty to ninety percent
of your thoughts and ways of emotion;
beg, or borrow, but cross the ocean.
Live a year if you possibly can
in Italy, France and/or Spain,
where the light – take this on trust from us –
though hard, makes objects luminous.

So, open your senses, let things seep
into the mind's absorbing deep.
There Africa and Europe will
coalesce and fuse until,
suddenly, out of your brain's abyss
will shoot the flowers of synthesis!

You see, dear Corduroy, unless
we modify our mental dress;
unless we clothe our minds and hearts

with home-grown images and arts;
and neither deny our heritage
(like adolescents come of age),
nor fail to grow new loves, and change
the down-side for the mountain range –
every single (snowless) summer
will find us bigger, dimmer, dumber,
till, like those clumsy dinosaurs,
we'll die, a race of thugs and bores;
and our tremendous African sun
will glitter down when we have gone
on others, less incongruous.

Love to Mimi.

Ever,

Gus.

THE UNDERDOGS: 1950

Against the ferro-concrete cliff
of the Stupendous Cinema,
behind bright chattering queues of fans,
motionless, four loafers lean:

black statues in the flurrying street,
statues of seamless diorite;
only their sullen eyes give warning
that such dark stones are dangerous.

You, who think a race will draw your water
and wash your dishes and dresses for ever and ever,
who wish they'd stay nice unspoilt kaffirs, forever
taking your orders on farms and mines,

look at these rebels! They have renounced
the nice obedience of the sons of Ham,
have joined, instead, the bitter tribes
of Ishmael and of Cain.

Look at them. Repulsive, degraded
and coldly self-assured. No glib tongue
smooths their speech. They have found
a danger-deep integrity. Look!

Terror of White suburbs, smelling of stale skokiaan,
smoking lip-sticked stubs of picked-up cigarettes,
waiting for night, the burglars' tart,
waiting for night.

This refusal to be menials,
this devil's pride in pits of crime and fear,
shall cry in crisis like a thunderclap
through midnight gales of yelling recruits.

Time, surer than the Stock Exchange
will pay big dividends to underdogs:
injustice, stronger than a Parliament
will grant red rights to underdogs,

to forget all terror in despair,
to marry violence with hope …
So what! We, of the chosen pigmentation,
shall calmly call on our tribalised God:

'Lord, save the shining Christian culture
of White South Africa!' Then squat
heroically behind clean Vickers guns
jabbering death in our innocent hands.

SUNDOWNER

Languid lady, whose head and sinuous arms
open like orchids from a night-shade dress,
within your cloudy synthesis of calms
flickers electric restlessness.

So shut the door, and draw each curtain shut.
Turn up the hissing gas, and dip your mind
in loosening gin; slur on your tongue sweet smut,
smart art; but at all costs, stay blind,

shut the dark cell at your Siberian centre,
the steel-ice lids that keep the soul's eye blind:
its dimmest blink upon this glitter-banter
would cockatrice your loveliness to sand:

the Eye that like a holy Russian moron
strode uninvited through your favourite room
and pointed to the mirror. Though the Gorgon
hissed sharply through your fresh cosmetic bloom,

it failed to freeze the hero on the shingle,
that grim, slack-bellied Perseus of the poor.
To save your face you simply had to strangle
a rickety kaffir brat and a half-caste whore

who begged across your boudoir in his wake.
Their corpses rot within your scented peace.
The Eye's in prison. A cool possessive snake
slips patient coils around your precious fleece.

So shut the door and draw each curtain shut.
Flaunt wide the peacock-eye-fan of your mind,
and pray for the day your scarlet nails will cut
the Eye right out: then you'll be blessed, blind.

GAME

As in the shimmering wake of a thunderstorm
calls or carols from airy or hidden birds
will underscore the stillness of the bush,
so words after love, caressing or mocking words –
like gleams or sunbursts on a level sea –
carelessly stress an elemental calm:
great passion spills into a pristine hush,
a hinterland that mocks mere history.

Even at trampled waterholes among
the nervous crowds who, listening, frieze the brink
then sip at life dyed dark by blood and dung,
lovers will saunter as if through Eden: mild,
insouciant as lions, stoop, and deeply drink,
knowing their wells can never be defiled.

PATIENCE

Quite ineluctable, my love like light
can't soften the clear hard shadow it throws
upon these oversimplifying snows
left by our sudden storm-tormented night.
In love's mild latitude such monochrome's
unnatural, cannot last. A born fool knows
that under zero's quilt big rainbows doze,
that brilliant music sleeps in tacit streams.

But if my simple similes are false,
this pallor permanent, your rippling pulse
levelled to a dead-beat metronome,
Darling, I love you still; be sure all through
your frigid solstice I'll keep hearth for you,
I'll kindle coals: when you are cold come home.

DAVID

You pure and nimble boy, like candle flame
burning above the pebbled brook, you'll bring
far more than wild doves tumbling down off wing:
bronze-armoured giants shall crumple in your aim.
You shall be King, and Lion:
out of your stripling flesh shall flower
majesty, dominion, power
and the salt, white walls of Zion.

Bathsheba shall break you. Long histories
shall hear your heart-beat leap and break in your rhyme:
oh, they'll forget your laws, your feats of arms,
but not the hour when with aching limbs
dragging up steep stairs, your aimless eyes
weep stones for all the Absaloms of Time.

COMMUTER

Perhaps at dusk in an empty moment
when trees move massive against dark skies,
neglected novel across your knees
head back, oblivious to all the noises
the rhythm of rails, earth spinning
towards black hills on the horizon,

at such a moment you might remember
no clear picture in time or place
people, accent, colour, texture
but the first flush of being together
how the heart beat then, innocent
love in a wood where tigers wandered
tame to our touch, burning for our delight.

Keep the moment in suspense, hold it,
welcome the autumn leaves arranged in the hall
and children tumbling on tiger skins
safe on the cool and polished floor.

HOME THOUGHTS

I

Strange rumours gripped Olympus. Apollo's hand
paused at its work, set plummet and rule aside;
then glittering in clean-cut bronze he sped
to rout the brash disturbers of that peace
which year by year had raised archaic Greece
nearer his vision of the poised and planned.
O barbarous with drums, with dancing drums,
amid a snarl of leopards through whose hide
shimmer disastrous stars, the drunkard comes,
black Dionysus roaring in his pride!

Ten thousand times they fought, wrestling before
both gods and men; it seemed the very rocks
watched those wild bouts among the barley shocks,
the brown vineyards, the dusty threshing-floor.
If pressed, Apollo side-slipped to the sun,
striking his rival blind, while he in turn
would slink instinctive into copses, run
underground like roots, and hoot weird scorn
from his nocturnal world: but neither could
conquer the force in which the other stood.

The spectacle gave poets double sight;
their nerves grew keen to catch at brightest noon
rumours of drums; in dark, dream-burdened night
could wake to shafts not quivered in the moon.
At last, at Delphi, half in love with him,
Apollo gave the drunkard elbow room;
but though his pride of leopards purred, near tamed,
and he himself grew decorous, he might
still breathe a deep, vibrating gloom
round anything the Bright One named.

At length, when peasants through his autumn trance
stirred slow pavans for summer on soft drums
he cried aloud (his leopards stretched their limbs):

124

Kill me, Apollo, or join the tragic dance!
Instead the Bright One watched: the flexing knees,
the raving, rending; heard the ecstatic crying;
but mirrored on his mind's white dancing-floor
dark dancers sighed and swayed like cypress trees
around a man on whose defiant dying
cracked clouds of knowing never moist before.

II

Why do I hanker homewards, falter?
Because in Arno's flood the stars
cavort with neon signs, headlights of cars?
The Centaur, snapping its human halter,
demolishes baroque façades;
the Great Bear runs amok
among our maps, tugging the Pole awry;
oh, all things heave and buck
since Dionysus slipped Apollo's guards
and let his leopards range the earth and sky!

Stupid of me to brood and cry
these barbarous confusions where
triumphant marble effigies defy
the moody turmoils of the air;
but, as at home, I here discern
the predatory shade;
asleep all day in ivy or that fern
which smothers the balustrade
it sniffs the night and pads the cracked parterre
between dry laurels and the shattered urn.

Man's task is to get such dark things clear.
Old Galileo, that empiricist,
through gothic tombs, antiphonies of psalms
smuggled a serpent-sharp idea;
smooth linen cordage looped in his swinging fist
chilled the ascending stairs;
the sceptre-grasping icons round the dome
shook as his ape-like palms

payed out that system-smashing metronome
whose jazztime spoilt the slow waltz of the spheres.

Long years drifting though African dark
bred dreams that I might find, once here,
a burning beacon, a gyro-setting mark –
that cord would ruck and tangle where
the rough stone of a leopard's bark
ripples the scrub with fear.
What pendulum can trace the mind's unseen
sharp arcs, its blind man's reach
round knots of being that have never been
subdued to slip through flaming hoops of speech?

Never so clearly have I known
that though the sharp mind's eye was made
to sever struggling shape from strangling shade
these shapes and shades cannot be mine.
My African creatures, across this night
I glimpse in our primitive storm
of thunder, whirlwind, mirage-twisted light
a lifted limb or glance
which I might free, give consciousness and form
dared I but stare into your furious dance!

III

Old Galileo's heirs can cite
how stubborn atoms may become
open to change in unimpeded light,
or round a rod of platinum
may curtsy, open arms and start
dancing a different dance;
but the catalyst remains itself, apart,
waits like a hermit there
through dull khamsins of accident and chance
to set one crystal, get one colour clear.

These images at which I stare
beneath such slow, myth-burdened stars,
Virgilian forests shedding mortal tears,

might blind me in my native air.
Unless for some loved principle one strips,
as the desert fathers did,
the soul of gaudy accidents, and grips
a Mosaic serpent or rod
one's deepest cries come from Egyptian lips
blowing dead bubbles on a Red Sea flood.

I have not found myself on Europe's maps,
a world of things, deep things I know endure
but not the context for my one perhaps.
I must go back with my five simple slaves
to soil still savage, in a sense still pure:
my loveless, shallow land of artless shapes
where no ghosts glamorise the recent graves
and every thing in Space and Time just is:
what similes can flash across those gaps
undramatised by sharp antithesis?

I boast no quiet catalytic wand
nor silently swinging, tell-tale pendulum
to civilise my semi-barbarous land;
a clearer love is all that I bring home:
little, yet more than enough. Apollo, come!
O cross the tangled scrub, the uncouth ways,
visit our vital if untamed abysm
where your old rival in the lustrous gloom
fumbles his drums, feels for a thread of rhythm
to dance us from our megalithic maze.

Nervous he wanders staring-eyed among
barbarous forms unknown to the northern muse.
Leaves, granites touch him; in ear, on tongue
new sounds and tastes, so many they suffuse
his sense with a blur of heat: delirium
that neither sleep nor sweat can clarify.
Oh, let the lightning of your quickening eye
and his abounding darkness meet and mate,
cleave, crack the clouds! From his brimming drum
spill crystal waves of words, articulate!

West Africa – South Africa
1954–1966

BRONZE HEADS, IFE, NIGERIA, 1954

I

Mud-mat villages like childish sums
all wrong on a slate; the bad road through the bush;
loud babies, frantic hens; in heat and hush
happy-go-lucky soft-mandibled drums
like termites at the pit-props of the mind;
then, foreign among smudged greens and dusty reds,
clear glass and concrete in a shapeless square,
this little museum. We find what we came to find.
Perturbed by their authority, we stare
in silence at the beauty of these heads.

Imperturbable, the kingly bronzes stare.
Their sudden resurrection from black loam
to our undisciplined light can't startle them.
Achieved for once, and so for everywhere
their tragic vision. These noble faces – faces
that felt time's touch and faced our common doom –
how passionately passive they glance at all
this rabble and rubble on their old high places:
such eyes might watch ten more Zimbabwes fall
and still outstare our continental gloom.

How can Zimbabwe's walls and these bronzes sum
our continent's long tale of joys and tears?
What sage grew wise behind her hedge of spears?
Wood carvings are made for white ants to consume:
small skill in friezing life, no glazing breath
to fix in art, as did the calm Chinese,
those seconds of sight that make a fool of death.
While Troy and Rome were towering, tumbling
and dead Cordelia weighted the old king's knees,
here only the sun-warmed granite was cracking, crumbling?

Sixteen centuries since the Cross, and none
have paved a highway, keyed a bridge, or arch
through which victorious regiments might march –

no ringing of trowels down on neat, dressed stone.
Through plains as large as Europe floes of game
went drifting on the droughts, and lost tribes wandered
changing their plumage like migrating birds.
Young men were brave; no doubt the old men pondered –
vague ghosts in footloose air, since no scribe came
to pen their deeds in palisades of words.

My eyes are staring into their brazen stare
but mind's absorbed in a long-lost Southern scene:
an old surveyor's tombstone skew between
rough stems of scrub invading the burial square;
it seemed the ancient, unmapped world had won:
all round mimosas foamed; a dancing wind
with bees and birds upon its drunken breath
with golden blooms and white thorns shook the sun
whose saffron light and blurring shade made blind
the lucid name and date-line cut beneath.

What trees more apt than these to symbolise
undated cycles whose proud rituals of war,
first fruits and making love once froze before
the timely wisdom in this bronze king's eyes?
But dreading what subtler dances might be born
within his wisdom's shade, rebellious sons
blinded and broke and black loam smothered him.
And still the sap of tribal trees all runs
to lavish dithyrambs of golden bloom
or Spartan regiments of long white thorn.

II

Far south: In wagons my folks bore
barrels of gunpowder and the Book of books;
found all things different: language, looks,
concepts of property, law;
no preaching steeples, signposts, watching maps
keep frontiers prim: the exile's fist must clutch
bare acres and hours in unique acts.
Small wonder, pitched between drum-shaken rocks,

felling the scrub, or fording cataracts,
that they were forced to jettison so much.

Wakeful round their red watch fires
while war chants surged between strange stars and veld
they found the love of God less clearly spelt
than in the neat and bell-blessed shires.
Frontiers turn justice rough.
Men kill for a home. In history
all but the saints must take their kid-gloves off:
yet when they met upon the Sabbath day
each granite torso, softened, seemed to pray:
'Deal gently, Lord of hosts, with such as me.'

Their women by old instinct knew
the not-so-vain importance of their clothes,
of fashions, graces, quieter prayers, small oaths
to cool the breath their menfolk drew.
Victorian bonnets snubbed the stone-age sun:
full sleeves and fuller skirts, pink frills, blue laces
kept visible still the delicate vein.
Their treble part-songs touched the wilderness,
unleashing over coarse and arid spaces
a thistledown attack of gentleness.

III

The first year they built cattle kraals:
next, hacking acres clear of mimosa thorn,
they ploughed and put them under Indian corn:
then quarried stones for their homestead walls.
You smug inheritors of landscapes where
each gentle acre praises long generations
who taught it what clothes and when to wear;
O heirs to bridge and byre and buttressed wall,
imagine that chisel chipping, those first foundations,
brand new, without a precedent at all.

But more significant by far
than this migration of an English hearth

132

rose Northern shadowy trees from the alien earth
to soften this Southern wedge of star.
As odd disturbances of air or light
(halo, rainbow, cross-wind or eclipse)
may herald a hero in disguise,
so, dwarfing the mimosa's gold and white,
these trees might be our green apocalypse,
artesian shimmerings under arid skies.

Wide winds that rifle and disperse
the airborne seeds of my subcontinent
had never frisked such stately stems nor bent
leaves so abundant and diverse.
The strict Euclidian sandstone hills
who'd kept unsmudged their classic forms
through patient centuries of scrub and bush
saw in those shapes an index of new wills:
ears keener to catch the lapidary hush,
hearts twice as stubborn at the heart of storms.

Roots in a fossil dinosaur,
housing all day a wise and constant owl,
the dark pine dulled the hunting-dog's mean howl
as it had dulled the wolf's before;
stood steeple-fast against the glare and gloom
when rumbling tribes poured lava on the farms.
All this was old. A straight-grained stem,
which demi-gods had smoothed for mast or spear,
might justly weigh in green perennial arms
tempestuous seasons of a younger year.

Subtler, the poplar caught whole shoals
of singing migrating birds, and let them go;
then vainly stretched bare seines for the knowing,
slow constellations, those peripatetic schools.
This too was old. She knew all distance made
to reach across; and torn things more at one
in Sheba's laugh than Solomon's fine frown:
but now she trembles, lest, beyond her shade,
bright children dancing in the scented sun
should join the watching regiments of thorn.

IV

Few tribes chant now; and hearth-rug lions are dumb;
Most rivers and ranges are mapped and properly named;
but Africa is anything but tamed
and God alone knows what is yet to come.
In spite of city parks and private planting
there's little shade for the contemplating mind:
yet though old drums, beast cries and racial ranting
raise Cain in the thorn-scrub rising round our hearts,
the naked eye, still steady, bright, resigned
must check, cross check, each reference on its charts.

If, having made a fair and heart-felt choice
to plant ancestral, shade-endowing trees,
the back must bend, yet on rebellious knees
the heart has cause, and cannot but rejoice.
For when the tribal energies, the flames,
the golden sap and blood revive, reform,
and dance down ways the staring eye discloses:
when shapes long stifled in our sensual storm
strike free and chant their clarifying names,
who will grieve at the strain such work imposes?

O brazen heads at Ife, you who stare
over the jungle, down the cataract,
as if such staring were the first slow act
by which man masters chaos anywhere,
stare at me, you bronzes, stare, persist
till, having caught your straight, incisive gaze,
I cut the scrub with calculated glances:
stare, as I replant, on dazzling days,
ancestral trees; stare on my sweating fist
in which, this moment, your bloodstream dances, dances.

ALOE AND MIMOSA

My own trees have no history,
no Christ or Caesar enjoyed the shade
of their niggardly foliage,
were not in Eden or Babylon's garden,
no poet or painter ever made
them part of my western heritage.

Far from the central, seminal sea,
on this earth's gaunt periphery,
they raise thin timber out of stone
and challenge a savage sun.

Golden mimosa mostly grows
a thicket of black stems,
each green leaf protected
by a twin of long white thorns.

Each year each aloe thrusts
through rings of dying leaves
a stem that bears new green
and scarlet like a crown.

Scarlet and gold in my heart of hearts
they twine their roots around my bones.

GROOM: GIRAFFE: EMPEROR
(from a 15th-Century Chinese painting on silk)

Both sceptical and superstitious the black-bearded groom
can't quite believe that his foreign charge is real,
except when, as now, instead of lolloping after,
it fixes all four feet in their tracks and jerks
that long neck back. The long rein, losing its slack,
almost dislocates his clavicle.
So he turns, this stocky groom, turns in his tracks

135

to utter an oath both bestial and blasphemous;
which oath has a long way to go, all up the long rein
to reach those ears perched like birds
on the heaven-high head –
that sensitive nostril sniffing down,
thin lips curled to reveal teeth gnashing,
long-lashed almond eyes in a questioning frown –

that fine, intelligent, highborn, foreign face
objecting to being led by him, him, chief groom
to the Emperor-of-all-the-Chinas.

Surely the merchants supplying the royal menagerie
have over-reached themselves, have gone too far this time,
to Africa, yes Africa,
returning with this – this? – this?
Is it an animal, or a god?
Either? neither? both?

I know about animals, I do, says that groom,
but as for you, you bastard between a camel and a leopard
with your hide all hidden in sinister hexagons –
why, if a god, did you get your divine self caught?
to amuse yourself with the sight of mortals
pretending to be gods? But if you're merely a beast
God help us both if you curl that lip
and sneer at his Celestial Highness.
Give me a hungry lion any day.

The celestial Emperor looked long at the long creature
three times as tall as a man, and then he said,
It is the holiest of beasts, its head being closest to heaven,
it is sweet of soul, its hide is a golden honeycomb.
Let it be fed forever on vegetables from my gardens.

How long did the African exile survive, bored,
stiff-necked from stooping
to a diet of fresh imperial greens?
Did he dream of days when he'd gazed at the sun
rising over a sea of acacia tops,

ignorant that it was already setting
over this imperial menagerie,
these staring crowds, these makers of lucid porcelains,
this delicate painter on silk?

LIVINGSTONE CROSSES AFRICA: 1856

I

A century of smoke since Livingstone
with Bible-stories, beads and bales of cloth
struck through the darkness under Capricorn
the slow white lightning of his westward path:
the sextant shook so in his feverish fist
that roughest bearings were impossible;
homesick, his bearers champed; his bridling will
grew brittle snaffling bouts of mutiny;
and then one morning, blue through the torrid mist
there broke the long Te Deum of the sea.

The startled bodies of his bearers stopped
dead in their tracks. Indeed he had not lied,
for there, beyond the forests, gleamed and lapped
a thousand broad Zambezis multiplied
by all the leaves on every African tree;
and soon they sang, (and would sing) to their friends:
'Oh, we believed old men and tales were wise,
that world goes on and on and never ends;
but we have walked to where the tired world cries:
Look! I am finished! There is no more of me!'

And when they reached Luanda, though he found
no letters waiting from the world outside,
shaken by fever and longing, he unbound
his diaries and wrote; and while the wide
banana leaves and breaker-dizzy birds
beat slow time to the boasts of his chanting braves,

137

he poured new-smelted facts of plant and beast,
of symptoms and diseases, trade in slaves,
the vast escarpment's tilt towards the East
into a cast of grey, laconic words.

But times out of mind his eyes betrayed his pen
and, desperate with forbidden love, leapt free
to the outside glare, to focus quick, and then
went rifling the tropical muslins on the sea.
There, dark, dry, neat as a chrysalis,
the British cruiser swung upon her chain,
ready to uncrinkle wings and skim
oh, into what complete antithesis –
shapes, scents, sounds bred in his bones and brain,
roadways, landmarks, temperate airs of home!

Hot winds between pulsed with his bearers' boasts.
Since none could take them home if he were gone
he wrenched his grey gaze inward from those coasts
to threadless labyrinths of scrub and stone.
Trusting long letters to those sails, he turned
and led them back, now docile to his grip,
singing of huts by which slow dung-fires burned,
of grass so tall the cows stray miles apart,
singing the sea, white wonders, and that ship
whose anchor dragged for years across his heart.

We can but guess at what fixed times and places
he set the sextant of his intellect
to exorcise those mirage-haunted spaces;
or what great deaths it cost him to detect
one fact grown trite among our daily speech;
but three thousand miles away, two years
and he flings down on Quelimane's beach
more ingots hammered from his forehead's forge:
the world applauds, but louder in his ears
the Smoke that Thunders, Cabora Bassa Gorge.

II

Deeds of the great possess the power of myth
to clear the image small men hold of themselves.
Suddenly they quit their niche in Death
breaking their stiff-spined sepulchres on shelves,
and, leaping Space and Time, stare at us, pour
a flood-light round our lives. And so on me,
beachcombing this sophisticated shore,
now that the scales have crumbled from my eyes,
his first great journey shines and lets me see
my travails dwindle to a decent size.

Nothing is as expected now I am here;
no reassurance of a heart in heaven,
no letters, no hope, no home; and yet despair
is bearable. I live, and there is even
a certain joy to find the heart so tough.
Meanwhile my bearers, blood and bones,
the tribal flesh that often cried, Enough,
now that my searching ends in a sudden sea
squat on the shore and croon in undertones:
'Look, you are finished; but there is more to me!'

I have no data to write up, cause to promote,
yet resting at earth's edge my fever dies.
What then shall I do? Sit here and rot
among these strangers, listen to the lies
my lazy bearers bring, and let my wit
run rank to sterile seed? Or shall I turn
back to my own world, examine it
with eyes that have their vision at command,
eyes that note with care, and do not yearn
for lights that never were on sea or land.

This, this is my discovery! I shed
a tangled jungle from my straightening shoulders,
I hack down the ju-jus in my haunted head.
Between these quiet, quenched volcanic boulders
I have come to terms, expect no wonders,

heart-easing revelations; but Space and Time
in staggering calendars of stone, real thunders
of clouds and streams, and I, without self-scorn,
noting what passes between myself and them,
whether in Naples here, or under Capricorn.

III

I turn in the dusk and mount the terraced slope.
In front two workmen, far too tired to sing
divide their common burden at the top:
along the nave of sand two lovers swing
the censer of their love; a whistling child,
pausing, leans to listen how down the well
water drips in the dark. All strange, all wild,
so secret and distant in the severing gloom
they set my savage senses at a yell
for human bread they hunger to consume!

Each pair of eyes and gesturing hands
says something other than a field or street,
or prayer that begs or credo that commands –
a mystery my senses cannot eat:
this is the distance that I have to cross,
between the I and Thou: discovery
strange as a gorge, a beast, or waterfall,
at which I stare, am at a sudden loss.
The cold and noting eyes can see, can see
not leap the gaps which isolate us all.

NEAR HOUT BAY

Stopping the car, our childhood friends, now hosts,
suggested we stroll to the fabulous view.
Blinding sun, and heat beating up from a path
gritty with pinkish granite crystals,
curtains of pines permitting

140

expected glimpses of throbbing cerulean sky
and steep striated rockface plunging
through broken mirrors, torn lace, beautiful lawns of sea.

There had been much talk in the car, far less on the climb:
talk which, try as we would to make it heal or hide,
only exposed the gaps, unbandaged sentence by sentence
the gashes and wounds of time, great spaces and falls
between us all. Each thread of phrase drifted from lips
like a spider's web from a cave in a thousand-foot cliff,
out, out into distance, finding nothing to cling to –
the next land Buenos Aires.

We gave up the effort. They tried a bit longer,
stopped in mid-sentence as we all stopped moving
in the space and the heat
before the sufficiently epic view.

Silence took charge, a blessed burial of words.
Each forgot his failure, longing, boredom, fury
in that subsidence of even a pretence at speech.
We stood a long time, still, just listening:
ten thousand sun-struck cicadas ecstatically screaming;
near and far hundreds of doves in relays
imperturbably repeating themselves to each other;
pine wood sighing into the wind from a thousand shimmering
needles;
wind already burdened with the grumbling,
perpetual, unpitied,
crumbling of the surf.

Returning, the talk returned
but attempted nothing whatever.
What can be healed or hidden?
We accepted separation
as the ear those ignorant sounds
that filled that primitive silence
with sadness and with praise:
cicadas; doves; wind; surf.

FROM ELEGY II (1960)

In all of us two continents contend;
two skies of stars confuse us, on our maps
the long- and latitudes contort and rend
our universe to twenty-acre scraps.
Yet this dead man and I, though poles apart
in countless ways, could meet in quiet gaps
to marvel how a major work of art
from many warring worlds could conjure one
to cut calm orbits through Man's cloudy heart.

That same mounted day each sought to bind
his people's freehold to our no-man's-land
but found each title densely countersigned
as tracks round troughs or through damp river sand:
whose beacons claimed that valley? who first rode through
the barrier ranges that on either hand
set stony limits to our longest view?
Disputing on the old disputed frontier –
as if the issue were still straight and new –
suddenly both fell dumb: abruptly there,
but centering the veld for miles around,
six inches higher than the bushes, where
no landmark was except itself, an old grave-mound
packed with round stones lay square. Soft hoof-thud,
soft saddle-creak, no hint of other sound.
Slow movement through still space: that made it odd,
our mute approach to one who'd long before
quit all dimensions for the none of God.
No wonder that, relieved to see and hear
some other movement near that stunning grave,
we stopped to watch a clapper-lark's career:
whistling she climbed, then hovering, clapping, gave
to eye and ear a higher focus, then
whistling she climbed again: so wave on wave
of air she swam oblivious of the men,
the listening and the dead, earth-bound below,
till with a sad long whistle for amen
she dropped to the stone-still scrub. With a vengeance now

142

on every sense the stinging stillness tingled.
Cast bronze, cut stone, we stood. I do not know
how long. Your steed stamped, her bridle jingled.
We woke, two strangers. Immobile, we had moved
from tribal worlds to being sundered, singled.

OCCURRENCE

At Devil's Cataract
a damaged reed leans death-still, vague
in aeons of mist through dynasties of thunder.
Take-it-or-leave-it sunlight flashes
whenever the vapour thins.

On which drooping arm
two drops of water: one clear silver
distilled in the Japanese print of the leaves;
the other, stealing from soil to roots
an Abyssinian brown.

Seconds, ages apart
reflecting the mist, each other, the elbow
of broken cane between, the fickle light
would sometimes pierce them centre to centre
clean through their naked skins.

What pulled or drove them together?
Fear of roaring collectives of river?
The tug of contraries to touch each other?
Or something external? a breath of air,
a tremor of the world?

No matter. By fits and starts
then faster, together, until they touched,
rushed, kissed, fused to a smoking pearl,
flashed in an opportune gleam, rejoiced:
creation shone, magnificent.

Nothing changed on the earth
as that mixed meteor slipped and fell.
For less than a second the roar seemed older, louder
and in the mist, immobile still,
clearer the broken reed.

KEEPING A DISTANCE

I

Through such gentle comforts –
good food, good wine, a companionable room
lit gently
a dozen voices in various accents
conversing politely –
I hear dumb longings for old-world cities
gardens with statues, squares with fountains,
now curtained in iron, raped by guns.

O lost Eden,
childhood before the deluge rose,
before the exile,
medievally far in time and place
you press as close
as these originals on the walls:
dandelion Degas dancer, an acid
Lautrec, a cool scene by Cézanne.

No exile, and yet
to capture trembling in webs of words
a childhood remote
among shrubs, birds, granite and storms
I must take all
as lightly and as tenderly as these
proud Spaniards, gentle Viennese
their childhood in forbidden cities.

What beauty, what virtue
flower in clean-kept distances!
Artists and exiles
disciplined by fate and choice
may learn how to master
their times by Time, their places by Space:
without strict distance, no clear vision:
Babel breaks from a voice too close.

II

Into the room you sweep
earth-encircling American girl,
to show me your miraculous world
as a child shows a bubble she has blown
or a birthday balloon, excited,
afraid to shake it free
to try its luck in the air.
I see all in your eyes,
distance, dullness, iridescence
of 'planes among cumulus, white wakes on seas.

'How hard to put worlds into words,' you say:
'Skyscrapers, pagodas, houses on stilts,
and silks flowing over fingers
like water over weirs.
Leila is Persian for dove:
in a fairy tale
she beat his prison windows with her wings.'

At this point
your trembling world stands still,
glows clear as a pearl through the smoke that drifts
between my eyes and your open hand.

III

A Spanish guitar begins to beat,
two voices make love in the air.

How could we guess
that each while speaking
of distance and art
would suddenly stumble,
stand still, stare
at the other's unwritten immediate heart?
Dove at the prison window
Over the seas to the drifting ark.

IV

Though eyes drift over you as lazily as clouds
upon an island in an interminable sea,
though parted by your body for these moments
the dim flotillas of sense swirl quietly on,
my flagship is wrecked
on your shores of silk:
I stare at a hand like a shell
cupping a bubble or pearl.

Body so still, all listening lines at ease
yet rising through arm over stole, white shoulder, up
through the supple stem of your neck to a face which accepts,
unquestioning, the warmth and light of the song,
motionless as sculpture,
separate as a star,
why, dear dove, do you beat
my prison with soft wings?
Were I to touch your hand a circuit would close,
windows blow open, doors crash: a lightning flash,
singeing the walls, would scorch the rafters bare.
Alone on a blackened floor, nervous at first
we'd move in tune to the song;
then, distances drifting away
like festive balloons or bubbles,
we'd melt to a single centre.

V

Cold clocks will strike.
The guitar must go sleep on the wall.

146

It's easy to get fixed
in the acids of Lautrec.

So I hold back to keep
your listening form and face
in the pastels of Degas.
How could the dance go on?

Don't move, don't end
deliberate distancing;
keep out of time, avoid
starting a history,

permit each form, each face
apparently at ease
to relax for a space in space:
with no future, with no past,

only a perfect present,
impersonal, perpetual,
held by the discipline
of Paul Cézanne.

In the delicate shell of your hand
let the pearl of your world spin on.

A SCHOOLMASTER'S BURIAL SERVICE

I

Distinguished-looking stockbroker,
blue-jowled breeder of stock,
two judges, a recent bankrupt,
young wife wearing a smock,
African household servants
of three generations at least,
six businessmen, one typist,
a headmaster, a priest,

147

girls, mothers and grannies
of various silhouette,
a solid mass of prep school boys,
dim bully, prim teacher's pet,

all find themselves united,
quite unembarrassed, at one,
in a cold church, at an odd hour,
out of the first spring sun.

II

Imagine – if a holiday crowd
were suddenly to hush,
stare in unison at the sea,
and all, all hear
the effortless roar –
something like that has happened to us.
We have lost, then found ourselves
way beyond ourselves.

Death's blinding, purging blend
of grief, affection, awe
has drowned distinctions of generation
in this formal end
of one man:
parent, schoolmaster,
master, friend.

In the bare and resonant ritual
his life for the first and only time
seems utterly articulate.
As time is devoted to his death
he lives, reflected and refracted
in the eyes and the memories
of our motley flotsam of heads.

'His life was gentle.' Gentleness,
spear-sharp, pierces us all. For once
there's compassion enough to spare
for the drier acres of grief.

Before we return to the first spring sunlight
and the splintering world outside
unbroken trebles rise like terns above
the rolling bass of waves that break forever,
lifting into the air for a little his favourite hymn,
sung at his own request:
'The day Thou gavest, Lord, is ended.'

Indeed, such gentle darkness
must fall at His behest.

IN MEMORIAM, J A R, DROWNED, EAST LONDON

This brilliant boy was stupidly drowned
while his parents watched from the beach,
his special body never recovered
from the indiscriminate sea.

Shrug your shoulders, sigh, say
accidents will happen; try
a little compassionate speech:
it's hardest on those who have to stay.

He was going into the Church.
And there's such a shortage of priests.
Then Who left whom in the lurch?

God loves
in such a mysterious way
sigh, say:
we can't understand His moves.

This boy was here on holiday
from Cambridge, where they say
he disciplined his tongue
to most incisive acts of prayer;
in agony for us here

where light after light is dowsed
he gathered a group of friends
to intercede for his and our land.

What on earth has this to do
with this butterfly-brilliant holiday crowd
drowsing near-naked in salty sand?

It's not much use to look wry, to say
we didn't ask for his impudent prayers;
whether we like it or not, forget or remember,
each Friday across this indiscriminate sea
his friends still pray for us, pray,
lift this landscape of separate beaches
into the indiscriminate light of heaven,
and hold it there.

For one who never set much store
by the efficacy of prayer
this legacy left to a drowsy country
blind in its easy dreams, left
by a dead boy, stupidly drowned,
wrings the mouth from its usual clinch
to tremble at the corners.
Staring at the indiscriminate sea
the eyelids blink to dismiss the impertinent tears.

Boy, young man, even
if there is no heaven
(I stand where your parents stood that day upon the beach)
continue to lift our drowning forgetfulness up,
teach us to look twice at every sea,
to discipline our speech,
to cry, to pray
incisively.

MENS SANA

His pet philosophy was
'There's a knack in everything –
in handing out whatever
one has the power to give,
be it a box of chocolates,
or a straight left on the chin,
in scoring points, whatever
is bowled at one by a screwball
tricky-wicketed world ...'

So, after a day at Newlands,
blue sky still in his eyes:
'All education's that:
poise of body and mind,
learning to handle your bat.'

Well spoken, elegant,
balancing on a cane,
making delicate passes
at gorgeous fashionable girls,
his secret passion was
to shine as the dreamt-of stranger,
the destroyer in their eyes,
obliterating in a tumble
their poise of body and mind.

He might have continued long
the dandy of education
till time or force of gravity
cut him down to size;
but in his prime
he met his match.

He fell disastrously in love
with an almost fatal *femme*
who knocked him for several sixes,
then left him publicly sprawling
after a hopeless catch.

That inelegant fumble
sent him stumbling to find
a point of balance somewhere
outside body or mind.

No longer a hit
with the herd instinct of the school;
can't play clichés pat
with crisp conviction or style;
annoys the Conformers' Club
with radical asides;
stays too long in the pub,
is tolerant of queers.

His latest gaffe was to ask the Head
after the routine morning prayers,
'Do you really believe in God?'

INTERRUPTED LETTER, FROM HOSPITAL

Dear Friends, in the craft and mystery of words,
most speech is mere noise countering noise,
while song assumes an absolute stillness;
for or against nothing at all,
is needed by no one except the singer
who may, sometimes, be overheard.

Under brilliant light
needle pierces vein.
Instruments sparkle. Voices
echo. One is alone.
Star-dark timeless
stillness floods
the healing theatre's
stage and wings.

Ready with words
precisely chosen
rehearsing each delicate
hand's precision

surgeons sisters
masked remote
wait to enter
on my mock death.

Friends in the craft
remember once
our eyelids closed
the better to hear

exactly chosen
words in sequence
call into being
stillness glittering

singing moving
white remote
perfect within
a cosmic poise.

Friends, I am surer than ever,
I invite you to overhear:
though it's against our mortal habit
not to shout in the face of noise
let us always sing
sing in the presence of absolute stillness:
a verse, given that audience,
has been, is, and will be heard.

PRIDE OF PLACE

Returning home for lunch he flung himself
into his easy chair, then struck his knees
with his fists and groaned, 'Shouldn't we emigrate?'

She looked up from her sewing: 'What's up now?'
'I don't want to tell you this but I feel I must.
After my lecture on Conrad a third-year student

asked to see me and through monsoons of tears
confessed he was a spy.' 'For MI5?'
'Nothing so posh. Our very own Special Branch.'

She put down her book and lit a cigarette,
then smiled at him. 'Is Conrad dangerous?'
'All good writers are dangerous to thugs.'

'What on earth can he tell the Branch about you?'
'He tried to say but was bubbling so wetly I failed
to get the drift. They give the poor kid an allowance.'

'But why you?' He shrugged. 'Not only me,
there's Bright, du Preez, young Bishop and myself.'
She picked up her sewing. 'And why are you last on the list?'

PROFLIGATE PARSON

Once God's, no man
can ever withdraw:
Heaven will use
the frailest flesh
to underpin
the moral law.

White Man of God
caught in the act

154

with a daughter of Ham,
dumb now, unfrocked,
you shout against
our holy sham:

'With neighbours, whom
(to please the State)
we fail to love
as Light commands,
darkness dooms us
to fornicate.'

GREAT-GREAT-GRANDMOTHER

Bolt upright, reading her Bible for hours
in a wicker chair on the front stoep in the winter,
in summer under the pepper trees whose lacy shadows
wavered over the lacy shawl,
drawn tight across her little brittle shoulders.

When her sight grew dim someone might read to her –
but deafness following shut that door.
So then she'd sit there, crocheting for hours
by a remnant of sight and what sense of touch
was left in fingers as dry and shiny as silver leaves
freckled gold and brown.
But mostly her hands lay limp in her lap
except for occasional desperate twitches
which shook the shawl round her shoulders,
the shawl with which she seemed to shelter
her loneliness like a deformity
from a frightened and frightening world.

Alone. Husband and all her own children gone:
living among the noise of children's children
who found it hard to come near the awful
weak-eyed eagle of a race now almost extinct.

Sometimes, though, one of the wives in fumbling compassion
would make a child ask the old, old lady for a story.
She seldom obliged, reluctant to switch her mind
from her beginnings and endings to theirs.

But when she did her stories were mostly biblical
where the miraculous burst into the matter-of-fact
and the weirdly wonderful was all mixed up
with things a child could see at once
were as they always are.

Or sometimes she'd talk of pioneer days, long treks,
locusts darkening the sky, assegai wounds
that would only heal to herbs that the Bushmen knew,
the coffin always ready in the loft, the frequent
births, betrothals, burials.

But rarely of her childhood over the water, among
hills called the Cotswolds, of things we never knew, like snow,
like chestnuts, and nightingales, whole hillsides
deep in perpetual lawn with not a stone to be seen,
trees, without thorns, as high as the house, things
as lovely, strange and barely credible
as chapters in the Bible.

Each sundown her custom was to go for a slow, slow walk
along the selfsame track that had brought her there
three-score and all but ten years before,
her long mauve gown trailing a whiff of lavender
through miles of heady mimosa groves,
her cheek far softer and smoother
than any wild petal or fruit.

I was a young savage then, forever
chasing rats and lizards with my catty.
Springtime it was – what passes for spring up there –
that gradual crescendo of heat with little change of colour,
that thorough desiccation of air
before the great clouds stride across the sky
meet growling, and sighing fall.

The blue-headed lizard flicked his tail
and my futile pebble clicked on his purple boulder.
Released from their fatal focus, my eyes drifted up
and there she was, not fifty yards away, stock-still, black,
next to a wild pomegranate, flaming yellow, intense
against the funereal mauves of the scrub.

Was she resting, or dreaming, or peering with lashless eyes
at that annual but always surprising outburst of yellow?
And then, behind her, I saw the whirlwind coming;
now lurching like an inspired dancer
who snatches a beautiful moment
from the verge of a hideous fall,
now stalking straight and poised
like the holy pillar of smoke that led the Israelites
into the Promised Land.

She did not hear or see it come.
It struck her and she was gone.
For a dizzy split-second I thought:
She's been taken up to heaven, like Elijah!
And her shawl spun out of the sky and settled beside me.
Was I Elisha, inheriting
her mantle of powerful pain?

But then I saw her dress like a gnarled old branch
black in the flame of the bush.

I ran up crying, trying to help her.
But she'd sized things up, as always;
she never lost her head.
'Go to the house. Fetch Thomas.'

In her fall she had clutched at the thorny branches.
That's how the palms of her hands were pierced.

She was three long weeks a-dying.

There were times when she struggled to speak,
but it was too late, tetanus being what it is.

157

They buried her between two thunderstorms.
The scent the damp earth breathed
from the parted lips of her grave
was neither bitter nor sweet.

I did not weep then;
it is now that I weep.

A PRAYER FOR ALL MY COUNTRYMEN

Though now few eyes
can see beyond
this tragic time's complexities,
dear God, ordain
such deeds be done,
such words be said,
that men will praise
Your image yet
when all these terrors
and hates are dead.

Through rotting days,
beaten, broken,
some stayed pure;
others learnt how
to grin and endure;
and here and there
a heart stayed warm,
a head grew clear.

TOURIST INSIGHT INTO THINGS

I've often thought, well, our big black underdog,
you can't expect to turn him into a spaniel
simply by feeding him sugar cubes, even
the very best sugar, the most refined.

And anyway, I'm sick of spaniels. Once
you have shed your British sentiment
for dogs and other animals, once you've felt
your own dark life-blood pulsing like a drum,
you'll find our big black brother has much, so much to teach
                                                    you –
because, you see, he's still in touch
with all the old gods in a way
that makes one wonder
why D H Lawrence wasted all that time
in Mexico and Down Under.

Africans, like their continent, are not dark
for nothing. Their darkness is alive.

Compare, for instance, the various ways
we and they kill beasts. No priest in the West these days
leads the heifer (silken flanks with garlands dressed),
to the efficient abattoir. The whole thing's done
by an hygienic machine. Not quite nice of course;
witness our treatment of butchers; but we take no moral notice,
the life of a calf not being sacred to us.

All over Africa all cattle are sacred
and the killing of a bull
is a ritual, a ceremony.

In a tribe that I know well
twelve of the best and glossiest young braves
are chosen for the task. Unarmed, naked,
they enter the kraal. The strongest glossiest bull
lowers a horn-span five feet wide at them.
Black, pink-palmed hands leap, seize,

wrestle the beast to its knees.
He bellows helplessly.
The more he bellows the better: fathers, chieftains, ancestors
remember the deep bull voice long after they have forgotten
that silly sophistication, speech.

Next, with courage and cunning, the young men
lift the left hind-leg over the left horn;
careened on its right side now
the great beast cannot heave itself erect.
Helpless, it bellows in throes, and its eyes
roll, roll, and its breath in spurts
blows up a smoke of powdered dung.
All round it sweating black bodies
glisten under the stinging sun.

The best of the glossy braves
with a specially sharpened assegai
now drops to one knee, and deft, quick,
slits the midriff open. Smiling ivory,
he thrusts his right hand through the diaphragm
right into the thorax, more than elbow deep.
The young men chant; outside the kraal
there is a communal clapping of hands by old and young
and a great wave of singing like a seventh breaker
rising, deepening, as the bull roars louder, louder.

The thrusting fingers and thumb
have found the titanic heart.
he holds a bull's heart beating in his hand.
Thrusting deeper, deeper, he finds
the root of life, root of the arteries, the aorta itself
beating out its dithyramb.
Blind in the dark bull body man's fingers seize and squeeze it
                                                    shut.
In the great beast, the great heart shudders, bursts.

While hills and echoes carry the bull's last bellow
to the last of the ancestors, the laughing-singing-clapping wave
tumbles, sparkles, spreads in bubbles and spume

through the veins and the brains,
the nerves and the bloods of all that is African
on both sides of the grave.

White settlers, of course, don't like this way of killing,
cattle not being sacred to them. And they haven't
imagination enough to be tolerant about it;
they call it barbarous; and no anthropologist as yet
has got them to understand.

GRAVE ROBBERS

I

The stable still had a cobbled floor,
bull horns set in the old lime-plastered walls
for hanging saddles and harness, and a long,
worn yellow-wood crib with rough iron hitching-rings
and a horse-shoe for luck nailed over the door.

Dad said that coach horses on the Kimberley run
had eaten their scented hay there
till steel and coal pushed them over the mountains.
That unleashed a feverish hunt
for hidden parcels of diamonds; but we found
sunk in the flour-fine dust in the rafters
nothing more precious than an old Martini-Henry
its sights corroded, a spider's white cocoon
blocking its black barrel, and eighteen seventy
visible still in the pitted steel near the butt.

The room became my museum.
Display cases: two dozen paraffin boxes
stored with everything the town and the veld and the rubbish
tips
could yield to the magpie hand and eye
of a piratical boy in those miraculous years
when every morning calls out,

161

Ahoy, there! Christo Columbus!
Or, more recently, Good-morning, Mr Darwin.

A spear and a battle axe, fine Mashona work,
bought by Uncle Charlie in an absent-minded fit
on his honeymoon up to the fabulous Falls.
Tail feathers pinched from the only peacock in the park
'With a cry that shivered to the tingling stars'.
A pair of mouldy old buffalo horns
pitched out of the local club
along with the old committee.
Both had presided over
the billiards, gossip and poker
of a couple of wars (one local),
half a dozen elections,
and epoch-making fluctuations
in prices of feathers and wool.
A piece of rippled sandstone which my teacher told me
had taken that particular shape
by particular conditions of wave and wind
on one particular day
in two hundred and fifty million years of days.
Butterflies, beetles, birds' eggs;
a fistful of coins brought back by heroic uncles
from German East and Egypt and France;
chocolate box from Mafeking;
shell splinter from Vimy Ridge.

But the present passion was skulls:
three domestic cats, two brace of dogs;
ground-squirrel, rock-rabbit, mongoose and jerboa;
blue monkey; baboon, with two-inch eye-teeth,
and an oblong horse's skull half as big as myself:
bles-, spring-, steen-, rooi- and other bokke;
but all the larger carnivores were missing –
no lion, no leopard, nothing more lethal
than a long-snouted jackal and a blunt-faced lynx.

Most serious gap of all, no bone of Man
except two teeth of my own

knocked out in an epic scrap
with Hansie van Rensburg over the latest flag.

Louis, my half-section, was in the throes
of his set-book *Hamlet* and his own
awakening histrionic talents.
Baboon's skull in hand he sighed,
'Alas, poor Yorick,' but gave it up.
'We gotta do better'n this,' he said.

'Tell me how,' I said. 'Here, help me
write labels for these eggs.'

We stole into the front room to filch
some visiting-cards whose ivory finish and size
made them ideal for labels, but saw
that Mother and our old cook Susan
were not to be disturbed:
standing at the window,
staring into the street,
as people in small towns stare
at processions of any sort:
this was a native funeral
forced by the flooded river
to take a four-mile detour
all through the white town
and over the concrete bridge.

A single European,
a priest in cassock black and surplice white
led the procession of men in respectable black
and turbaned women with large black-glossy scarves
with tassels over shoulders and white blouses.
Pushed by pall-bearers
through white-hot air
a small handcart
whose wavering wheels
squealed under the coffin's
immortal weight:
black, big, black,

it was all black and white
like a photographic negative
except for a single wreath
of blazing marigolds.

'Who is it, Susan?'

'Deacon Joseph Jali, Ma'am.
Aiee, aiee, a good man, Ma'am.
Aiee, 'e was good.'

'Of your church, Susan?'

'Yes, Ma'am, yes. Baptise' me, my children
de leeving an' de dead.'

II

Jali, a far-off cousin of pagan Nongqawuse,
the girl prophetess who persuaded her people
that killing all cattle would call their dead chieftains
in red clouds rising from the rivers at dawn
to sweep the white men back into the sea.

Then there was famine in the land.
The great grain pits were filled with dead men's bones
and the women's breasts were dry.

His mother carried him over the winter mountains
into the white man's world.
One morning she heard a sound she would later know for a bell
ringing across the frosty rocks and dead grass sharp as needles.
She had him baptised at that Mission
and called him Joseph
because there was corn in this Egypt.

The Lord was good to Joseph and blessed his work.
In his time he baptised thousands of his people
into the fold of the Lord.

Deacon Jali is dead.

Believing in total immersion
as practised by John in the waters of Jordan
he would stand waist-deep in the old hippopotamus pool,
the sun on his wet forearms and sweating, shining face
multiplying the sign of the Cross
on brow after cleansèd brow.

Deacon Jali is dead.

Doves descending from the sky
were more than mere Darwinian birds
come down from the hills to drink.

Deacon Jali is dead.

Baptising all afternoon
while the chanting rose
and subsided in waves,
a subdued musical thunder,
over the pear trees in bloom,
lucerne patches, old quince hedges,
Saint Peter's Anglican Church,
the Convent of the Sacred Heart,
and dominating D R C.

Deacon Jali is dead.

Over them all and up to the clouds and the kranses
red as the blood of the Lamb in the evening sun.

Deacon Jali is dead.

III

We promptly forgot the Deacon's funeral.
Our urgent days in a glittering stream
tumbled us forward through numerous landscapes
to a late afternoon south of the town
where boergoats graze on the stunted thorns.

We were nearing the place where, rumour said,
storm waters from a culvert under the National Road
had scoured a ten-foot donga
through the cemetery from end to end;

165

where crumbling butt-ends of coffins
stuck from the sheer sliced banks.

It must be said in mitigation
that we believed the cemetery to be old and out of use;
that we saw our venture as no more sacrilegious
than the recent expedition that unsealed,
in the sacred name of knowledge,
Tutankhamun's tomb;
that boys in the grip of a hunger will stop at nothing
when the risk lies somewhere over
their receding border of wonder.

Rangy wild tobacco plants;
spongy ash-bush in pink soil;
slate-blue Mexican poppies
in whose desiccated pods
seeds rustled like dry sand.

A thousand fish-paste bottles;
jam and marmalade jars
their only immortelles
glittering like an ash-heap
in the declining sun.

Talk died on our tongues,
our easy walking stiffened,
we trailed our guilty spades
like men with heavy rifles
stalking no-man's-land.

We even crouched a little
as if to be erect
were risky among those trenches.
A single jackhanger cursing
made the air go brittle
condemning us out of hand.

We never reached that donga.
Across our path was flung

a row of recent earthworks;
our sortie withered to stillness
before a bread-brown wreath
of shrivelled marigolds.

In the little Karoo wind that comes at sunset
Hamlet's hand ceased itching for a skull
and Darwin's curious candle fluttered, then went out.
For a moment or two between sunset and nightfall
Deacon Jali came out of his grave
alive with subdued terror and music
from the ultimate fold.

SWEET WATER

While packing gold butter, lace doilies, buck biltong,
spring chickens, frilled aprons, cut flowers, dried peaches
into the boot and back seat of the car,
Aunt Betsy, convener of twenty committees
and big queen bee of the church bazaar
barked gently at the garden boy:
'Boesak! Where's Master? Find him! Tell him
that we are waiting.' Then, smiling, to me:
'Just like your Uncle, selfish old dreamer.'

When Uncle Danby took the wheel,
his hands would hover, seize it, feel
it for tension like one who tries
the reins of a horse who sometimes shies;
his legs, once expert with stirrups and spurs,
had never quite mastered these brakes and gears.
As the clutch was released, the back wheels sprayed
the hens with a shrapnel of gravel; dismayed
they took to the trees, while parcels galore
rocketed on to the Buick's floor.
No word of comment from the old folk:
was this start normal? or beyond a joke?

In silence we sailed with white winter grasses
swishing the mudguards; silence, enlarged
by the drone of the engine, by a startled korhaan
rising, clattering, into the sky: silence
seeping from petrified seas in the sandstone, so huge
that when I opened a gate the squeak of its socket
sounded small and sharp as a cricket
where grumbling breakers smother the old Cape granite
at dusk when a long South-Wester falls.

'So you're going to 'Vahsity?
That's what they called it,
them Pommie Awficers
in the Bah Wah.'

He chuckled, remembering
accents and mannerisms
of elegant red-necked subalterns
whose blue-blood pedigrees
went back to the Battle of Hastings
rather than Eighteen Twenty.

' 'Vahsity!'

'Yes, Uncle.'

'Man, I only made standard four.
Dad called us back to the farm.
He had his reasons –
a run of bad seasons
locust swarms in the sky
dark as the day of doom –
oh, long, oh, long before
the ostrich-feather boom.'

At the word 'feather' Aunt Betsy's hand
unconsciously fluttered towards her antique hat.

Ironstone koppies like dead volcanic islands
rising purple and black from oceans of grass,
fawn-soft grass lapping the parallel shales
of mountains thrusting daring capes and headlands
from continents still hidden over either horizon.

168

And here and there, as light as a drift of flotsam,
a store, an avenue, a kraal or a farm;
or a new-shorn flock of merinos like a trail of spume.

Not far ahead the Kwaai River
trailed its tawdry fringe of mimosas across the flats.
Soon our red-road-ribbon
would cross the stream, on the brand-new causeway,
the pride of the district:
opened last month by our M P C
with a speets on nashonil prowgriss
followed by braaivleis and brandy –
oh, concertinas and moonlight
and singing of Sarie Marais.

'Along this road,
come rain, come shine,
my brothers and me
we drove stock to the fair.
What I remember best
was dust.
Man, I must
of swallowed a muid or two
of good Karoo soil in my tirne.
But there was also
the sweetest water.'

He ran his tongue round his bearded lips.

Approaching the river we saw the causeway,
concrete, white, with neat crenellations
like a Beau Geste fort fronting the river,
but wide enough for one-way traffic only.
Carefully he eased the car down the slope,
then, slap in the middle, switched off the engine.

Aunt Betsy sat up with a start: 'What? –'
'Man, when I was a boy,' he said.
'Danby!' she cried, 'We're half-an-hour late!'
His blue eyes quelled her.
'When I was a boy,' he said,
'we always outspanned for the night,

here, among these trees.
There's no sweeter water
in all the district.'

The way he said it, with a smooth small gesture
of the arm from the elbow with the palm flat, downwards,
sent the mind's eye reeling over
the whole Fish River catchment
down South from Dassiedeur and Daggaboer
in a great arc North to Teviot
and West-by-North to Spitskopvlei.

'But Danby dear, we're half-an-hour late!'

I don't think he heard her. Sometimes a greybeard
leaning, listening down the deep well of his years
turns stone-deaf to the fractional present.
Seventy winters through his bones
since first he stopped at Kwaai River.

At the end of the newfangled causeway
he clambered over the ironstone boulders
and strolled up the river bed to a bend
where seventy centuries had scooped a bowl
in the crazily cracked substratum of gravel.

Fringed with palest sand, a large pool in the blue gravel
with a fine and feathery dust upon it
and water boatmen tracing
lazy arcs and circles in the sun;
their legs, no longer than an eyelash,
were shaking the reflected sky and making
the far-off images of mountains quake.

I heard a crescendo of hooting
and pictured the chaos at the causeway.
But he was oblivious, busy with things that mattered.

On the sand near the water's edge
he spread his handkerchief and knelt.
I could hear his old joints creak.
Embarrassed, I knelt nearby.

'Now,' he said, 'you must first
blow the dust from the surface, like this.'

The floating film gave way like wax off apple skin,
the frantic water beetles scattered so quickly
they left the eye blinking at ripples and ripples only.

'Now scoop the water with your hand, but never,
no matter how thirsty you are,
swallow the first.
That's to rinse the dust from your mouth.'

He did so, spitting the water behind him.

'Now,' he said, 'now,
oh, taste how sweet it is.'

Delicately, three times,
the huge and trembling hand
cupped the sweet waters of the Angry River
to his lips, to sip it with a little noise
softer than the whirr of starling wings
from their nest-holes in the bank above us.

When we got to the causeway a dozen cars,
some hooting, were waiting; and old Aunt Betsy
sunk in shame and sulks. Unabashed
he lifted stiff legs on to the pedals
and said, with an ice-breaking twinkle:
'But don't you want to rinse your mouth, my dear?'

Laughter and fury broke together from her:
'When I was a boy, indeed! When
were you ever anything else?'

Turning he grinned at me. The blue eye said:
'Oh, she don't understand us boys.'

He's dead now, and I am left,
bereft, wondering
to what stream I could take whom
and kneel like that, and say:
Taste how sweet it is.

171

FARMER

That sandstone stoep, festooned with bits of biltong,
is the bridge of his liner. From there he pilots
three thousand morgen of good Karoo veld
through sizzling doldrums of drought and stormy good seasons;
barks laconic orders at the 'boys'
who, wringing stained hats in yellow hands,
cringe on the blue gravel deck three feet below him.

That Hottentot crew hold him in their hearts
as a bastard child of terror and love.

He drinks black coffee at intervals till sundown;
then brandy is brought, and he tunes in to hear
the news of the great nonsensical world; he ponders long
till the southeaster rises and rattles the bluegum leaves
across the pebbled stars, and thinks
of Abraham and of Job.

His unloved wife is large and sad,
an excellent cook, a compulsive eater.
One surly son is managing a distant farm,
biding his time; another, doing quite well as a butcher,
has married a new wife; his only shameless daughter
is living it up among the neon lights
down at the wicked Bay.

A caricature? Of course. It is equally easy
to embalm him in warm sentiment.

I found him intriguing, liked him more each visit,
but never quite knew why until I turned my gaze
away from the clean slow folds of the veld
and looked, as a painter might, acutely,
at the heavy body in old bleached khaki,
elbows on knees, the brandy glass
held by both hands in front of him, firm.

At first glance his eyes seemed like a hunter's,
every wrinkle and line from crowsfoot to frown
pointing towards the clear grey orbs, alert,
watching something loved but treacherous.

He stayed like that for minutes without a movement –
relaxed and calm, enormously strong in his peace:
no, not like a hunter; not like a Buddha either,
nor like a saint in ecstasy, although
his poise was absolute.

Some infinite assurance reached him through his eyes.
The arc of the horizon, that particular
configuration of ironstone and grey shale,
pale soil stippled with dark round shrubs,
red grass in seed shaking along the ragged ridges –
he'd taken all that he saw into himself
and found that it was good:
it was water and breath of life to him,
he drank and breathed the distance through his eyes.

Suddenly I felt ashamed as if I had stared
with the wrong sort of interest
at a praying child or stumbled on lovers
with all their defences gone.
I looked away, at what he was looking at.

And now I can never think of him
without the clearest vision of those hills,
nor recall those hills without seeing him.
From my public, urban world
their relationship seems real.

THE DRUM OF THE DEAD
A Venda legend

Our tribes played many musical instruments:
the Lemba plucked the *deze*'s well-tuned metal tongues;
the Tsonga rippled with pink palms or padded hammers
over elaborate xylophones with echoing calabashes;
many blew upon sable horns, kudu, or horns of impala,
or flutes of special bamboo from the sacred woods of *Tshaula*;
also the *tshizambo*, a double instrument

(one end of a wooden rattle of tinder-dry *ntusa pods*
is rubbed on the side of a bow strung with *mulala* leaf;
the end of the bow is held to the cavity of the mouth
which, adding resonance, emits an infectious sound).
But only the Venda possessed a drum of their fathers
carried countless leagues from a land of gleaming lakes,
a land of forests and fruits, innumerable moons ago,
till they founded their city at last in the mountains of Vuvha.

No one will build there now; even today the Venda
will not cross that site; for many miles around
in the dry time ears go stretched, dreading to catch
the throb of the ancient drum of their fathers,
drum of the dead, Ngoma Lungundu.

Impregnable walls of stone, houses also of stone,
in the midst whereof the drum's house stood, whose walls
were gleaming granite slabs, whose roof was of great beams hewn
from distant woods; and the king's house stood hard by.

The great king, Mwali, like the drum, was never seen
no one saw the king or the drum except the old high priest,
he, Dzoma-la-Dzimu, he, the mouthpiece of God.

The king's dwelling and the drum's dwelling were guarded by
                                                    plaited fences
where snakes with a head at each end kept slithering watch;
also by twelve lions, watchdogs of the king:
quiet, quiet they were, only rousing to roar
in praise of their lord when the drum beat,
drum of the dead, Ngoma Lungundu.

The years passed. In the time of my great-grandfather
the people split into factions so stubborn and deep
that even the voice of the drum could not unite them.
Brother plotted the death of brother. A dry time came.
For months no cloud splintered to spill its milk.

At last the councillors crept to Dzoma-la-Dzimu
with a train of lesser folk. First they danced the *tshikona*,
a solemn dance of the men to solicit ancestral aid,
danced slowly, with concentration, to soft, antiphonal song;
then, sweating, they bowed to the earth, and sighing, all cried:

'Ancestor Mwali, Elephant, bright Light of the land,
Great king, hear us, Guardian of the drum.'
Dzoma-la-Dzimu took the plea of the people
to the king's dwelling. The people waited, bowed to the earth.

In silence he returned, bearing the sacred stick;
in silence approached the drum's house, before whose door
he knelt:
'Ancestor, speak, Master of beasts and of people,
Omen of clouds, Lord of the skies, Voice of the drum.'

Alone, with the sacred stick, he enters the house of the drum.
He beats the drum gently so those afar cannot hear.
But the king's dogs, they hear, hear and rise to roar
their terrifying praise, the snakes glitter and hiss like seas.
Molten with dreadful joy the suppliants start to sing,
their ululations rise, the royal precincts resound.
The far-off tribesmen, hearing, thread vibrating valleys
with a blowing of sable horns, flutes, and horns of impala,
to the beat of bare feet dancing, rattle of pods round ankles,
bodies and voices and music together, coming closer and closer,
all voices and limbs and instruments obeying the roar and the
beat,
beat of their hearts and the deeper beat of the drum,
till all are chanting in all six valleys as one:
'We hear you, hear you, drum of the dead,
Ngoma Lungundu.'

Then spear-sharp from the sacred place one trumpet sounded,
and the feet stopped, and the voices, and the horns, and almost
breathing
as they waited for their king to speak the words of the drum.
Alone, aloud, the drum struck like a cataract, then stopped.

Through a stumble of echoes the king's voice rose up wailing
grim, high pitched and broken, then stopped.

Again the drum thudded a sharp stampede, then stopped.

Once more the king's wail rose,
interpreting for man and for beast the words of the drum.
But what he said was hard to understand, his voice
so old, so broken, and speech perhaps from the far-off land

of lakes, and forests and fruit; but each in his personal terror
strained his ears to hear his own heart's drum respond
to the words the drum of the dead had spoken through the king:

'Hear me, hear me, my children descended from my wives,
especially you princes, great ones all.
Because you have set my people one against another,
bickering ceaselessly; because you, yes you,
have flouted my laws and mocked my ways, I will afflict you.
I shall hide myself in the earth, and leave you the dry sky only,
I shall crack the earth apart and your cattle shall sink away.
O would you were the men I led so long ago
so many leagues from the land of lakes, and forests, and fruits.'

The people lay in the dust in terror and contrition,
many fainted, many died from these hard words of the drum.
Never before had Mwali the king spoken in such anger
through the means of Dzoma-la-Dzimu, mouthpiece of God.
The earth shook and groaned; from a black sky thunder roared;
the king's dogs whimpered, fled; the houses of shining slabs
crumbled to rubble, lightning splintered the roofs
of the houses of drum and of king, and fire and smoke and
                                                        darkness
consumed the drum of the dead,
Ngoma Lungundu.

Those who survived were a few, and of them but a handful
came from the houses of princes. In the grey light next morning
there was a calling of one to another, to come, and to look,
and in every household weeping. They gathered their mats
and pots and skins under the sliding shadows of vultures.
As they left that place hyenas and jackals entered,
for even the beasts had heard the words that Mwali the king
uttered through Dzoma-la-Dzimu, mouthpiece of God,
through Ngoma Lungundu, drum of the dead.

176

South Africa 1966–1975

A still Karoo twilight

THE DIVINE UNDERGROUND

Souls *in flagrante delicto* or *in extremis*
stretched on the rack or Cleopatra's bed,
you have no news for me,
me, not fit to tread
where hawk-sure men of the media
zoom lenses down on your limbs in spasm
or claw at your grunts or ululations
with glittering microphones.

No, I go hungrily slumming for those who wear
a habit of discipline on every gesture, armed
in still affection, steel-bright after years.

I find them poorly disguised as morons,
under distorting stars,
lost in their lands of birth, quite ousted by
smooth bastards or daughters in gorgeous gowns:
in the cold, in the shade,
like lepers, like untouchables, in whose eyes
our storms of guilt dissolve in their light of forgiveness:
they know what they have lost,
they guess at what they have gained;
divining an innocent justice, they endure
our grand and murderous razzamatazz
as if they were God's spies.

MOUNTAIN

On the brink of flying to Europe,
standing alone and still
where the edge of the great escarpment plunged to the plains,
fearful of further falling in a fallen world,
I tabled my little problem before the Mountain-maker,
the Fossil-preserver, Rock-eroder, Cliff-carver,
Evolver of countless species, saying:

These are my current vertiginous terrors.
Am I guilty of vainglory in mentioning them?
You alone can know if my hunger for poise is just,
know I am held from falling
by a tension of forces I can't pretend to know.
A move from here
may well precipitate a fall,
while even here I fear
the magnetic field is shifting.
Am I to go?

No thunder, of course; and the only whirlwinds
were small fawn spirals, earthbound ghosts of dust
drifting across the flats below. Fire? Yes,
in the sun, but remote, impartial as always.
I heard no still small voice; only the mountain silence.

For a moment all concern for myself dissolved.
With no effort I shed becoming, and history
slid like a leaden cope from my shoulders.
For a moment, a moment only
I was
on the rock
in the sun.

I came down from the mountain, unweighted
by tablets of law, more giddy than ever.
For two years and more
I have done my worst and my best.
History has grown heavier since, becoming no easier
and between me and that moment only
are several abysses, disastrous plunges
and a few savannahs and walks through orchards in spring.

Frequently now I catch myself off balance,
tempted to take the wings of the morning or dive
to the uttermost parts of the sea.
Perhaps that moment which refused so firmly
to be a turning point
should be the only point

round which my life should turn;
perhaps God is neither old nor young;
in depth or in height. He simply is,
and we,
when we accept Him simply,
are.

TEN MINUTES' SILENCE 1970

I

Looking hard
at this past century
my bloodshot eyes lose focus, blur,
then wince and shut.

Behind pressed lids
salty tears spurt hot
to sluice from each raw lens of flesh
Time's cruel grit.

II

These tears are not
idle. I name their meaning:
Isandhlwana; Magersfontein;
the Western Front;

I pause at each:
Belsen; Dachau; Dresden;
Hiroshima; Mau-Mau; Sharpeville;
and Vietnam.

To one dead man
from each, I give one minute.
Deep in my skull, behind shut lids,
their damp eyes glint.

III

After ten minutes of silence with these dead
I turn to our proper concern: the future.
My study echoes with Utopias,
clean citadels of words
built by gentle theorists
who would do justice to the best in man.
Citizens in those happy squares
are unrelated to our dead, their veins
pulse with blood in no known group.

Why do I flush
and in a cold sweat turn
from all such humane abstracts, crying
Not for me?

Dead eyes have scorched
those comforting prescriptions
for man's old cancerous tragedy
to common ash.

IV

Only the just
who know what beasts and nightmares
lurk in the gentlest heart, who do
not pass the buck,

they alone
will stem the slaughter, they
restore the world. Only the just
have Time in hand.

DREAM OF A BUFFER STRIP

I

on twisted strands of wire
a newspaper splits in the wind
hairy goats with gold eyes
nibble at blood-red rags

where are we walking to
through what half-lit spaces

dead grass glinting like needles
criss-crossed by dust-soft footpaths
as white and long as weals

the sun like scarlet fever
rolls scalding over the brim
three gaunt rough-skinned donkeys
lift long jaws to bray
black holes through the pallid sky

eyes an innocent ice-blue
under his pilot's cap
david livingstone
opens his pocket bible

in chapter one st john's
apocalypse we read
and every eye shall see him
also they which pierced him

i see through binoculars
our new jerusalem
galvanised-iron mirrors
reflecting golden sun
and all encircled by
a ten-foot fence steel poles
and glittering diamond mesh

182

from it zigs and zags
through dark red flesh of earth
a donga's panga gash
patched and bandaged in places
with ash and rubbish tips
pinned by broken bedsteads
rusty roofing strips

and as it crawls towards us
leak pools of yellow pus
stitched all around their edges
with coarse kikuyu grass
green suckers cling and catch at
our leggings and our boots

suddenly from the sky
a falling fountain of joy
rains on a mountain top
high laughter airy excitement
of boys at reckless play

an innocent river of jordan
comes romping through my bones
my son and his friends must be
playing cops and robbers
along the banks of our river

it isn't my son playing
in the panga gash below
five black piccanins
in nakedness and rags
four are squatting teasing
stag-beetles to make them fight
the fifth by himself at the drift
is gathering blue smooth pebbles
dropping each with a click
into an old jam tin

the wire Y of his catty
dangles by red elastics

from the lizard-shiny blackness
of his thin left wrist

he is the first to see us

at his animal cry
quick they forget their play
stare hard at us start sidling
out of our sight towards
galvanised-iron mirrors
reflecting the golden sun
all encircled by
a ten-foot fence steel poles
and glittering diamond mesh.

but number five stands firm

a catapult in hand
and pebbles at his feet
it's all happened before
it's going to happen again
he'll slip a blue smooth pebble
into the primitive sling

watch out i yell watch out
darting my hand to my forehead
cracking under the strain

but david livingstone
shakes his lion's mane
both of you are afraid
and fear well fear hath torment
says the word of god
moreover the child is ill

i look at the child again
i see or rather hear
what holds him lonely there
outfacing our giant faces
under a cent-sized sun

he has trouble with his breathing
hisses hard for air
look he's fallen backwards
limbs slowly snatch at air
an outsize upturned tortoise

i stifle a laugh of relief

the pebbles spill from their tin

enormous leaden ripples
circle the yellow pool

huge six-legged beetles
lumber into holes
like craters on the moon

II

footfalls receding cries
cries closer footfalls and then
mimosa smoke tobacco
smell of servant's clothes
acrid blackman's sweat

blind and terrified
stumbling on hooves not feet
nostrils distended wide
as those of a maddened horse
stampeding a crowded street

i force my eyelids open
find i am following still
the obstinate doctor down
a colossal breathing nave
huge black men and women
dark as a thunderstorm

why aren't they all dressed up
in traditional beads and feathers

why are they all in their best
second-hand white-men's clothes

at the end of the avenue
a ten-foot fence steel poles
and glittering diamond mesh

livingstone strides at ease
as if over highveld grass
it's all very well for him
he has a stethoscope
to show to the special branch

but where oh where oh where
is my permit my passport my pass

i follow their line of sight
i see what holds them there
like stone-age worshippers
at human sacrifice
that damned asthmatic child
how did it get entangled
so brutally in the wire

it hangs there like a wild bird
blown to its twisted doom
in the bright new wire-netting
of our Sunday tennis court

at the sound of our feet falling
it starts to struggle to hiss

be patient little kwedin
or you'll break your shoulder blades
wait the doctor is coming
the great white wizard from far
he'll place his stethoscope
he'll tap your lungs and heart
a snow-white ambulance
will whisk you away away

to a white bed set apart
and when you come back again
you'll smile with brave defiance
at all your old witchdoctors
all this moody crowd
will be grateful to western science

the mad old doctor's gentle
sunburned hands reach out
unpin the fluttering child
he does not take its pulse
nor tap its heaving chest
he lifts it up sky high
then lowers and kisses it
between its squinting eyes
in the name of the father once
in the name of the son that's twice
in the name of the holy ghost
three times he kisses it gently
there at the foot of our altar
our holy diamond fence

the sun dies in a cloud
there's a terrible tremor of earth

the child sparkles with laughter
a hundred thousand blacks
exclaim with a loud click tixo
and now they begin to sing
and straighten their rounded backs
oh shoulders straight heads lifted
singing bass and soprano
what danger is in this joy
this music pouring forever
zambezi of blood and longing
i sing with them with them
smiling i sing i weep
i sing like an idiot
with the singing old explorer
the crowd and the singing boy

what am i doing here
what doing singing here
nkosi sikilele
with a crowd of blacks me

the child jumps into my arms

just imagine the stink
if the press gets a photograph
of me in a pose like this

he kisses me wet on the cheek
with all the force i have
i heave i hurl him from me
as if he were a snake

rivers of song dry dead
blindness pours black rain
through which i hear their silence
a high inaudible hiss
far worse than any shout

oh let them kill me now
now while i know my whiteness
deep down is still intact

but nothing happens nothing
they leave me to sweat in silence
till i cry for a sound some sound
oh any sound to stop me
from finally going mad

it comes at last the sound
as if the child were still
an octopus on my skin
its choked asthmatic breathing
becomes as one with mine

i force my eyelids open

beautiful and clean
pretty as a doll
in a christmas shop at night
with golden hair ensnared
in our ten-foot diamond fence
hangs dead my son my son.

AYLIFF AND THE LEPERS

Wednesday, March the thirty-first, eighteen thirty

After attending my English appointment, I took
a circuit round some distance to visit the lepers
who live on the banks of the Great Fish River.

I had not been before. The sun was declining.
Passing through a wood of mimosa trees
I came upon them suddenly in a group
on the banks of the river, sitting before their house,
regaling themselves in the sun before the close
of day and the autumn cold should compel them to retire.

I must confess that I was filled with pity,
astonished at seeing such objects of misery.
Restlessness – they seemed unable to sit still,
kept rubbing themselves continually, and one
poor creature bordering on stupor
paying little attention to what was passing;
yet they consider their greatest suffering to be
their social isolation; what afflicts them most
the exile of the heart and not their rotting flesh.

I never saw anything like it, no, not even
in the sick-bays of the Navy, nor hospitals where I
have seen so many miserable sights, but none like these.
I now see why our Saviour in the days of His flesh
was touched to the quick by the lot of the leper.

Tuesday, September the seventh, eighteen thirty

At intervals all through the winter I have seen
the lepers who live on the banks of the Great Fish River.
Some call me a fool for wasting my time on those
whom the world has already forgotten, as good as dead;
others tell me it is not healthy, that I
might bring the disease from them to others; but
I cannot pass by on the other side.

Today when I reached the desolate place I found
poor Antje Rautenbach sitting alone. She seemed
strangely at peace. Moved by I know not what
I asked her to tell the entire company
what had befallen her. She said:
'I cannot utter what I feel.
The first that I felt in my mind was two months ago:
it was so strange and sweet, so costly, like gold
that I was afraid of being caught with something
that did not belong to me by rights and would
perhaps be punished for having it. These things
were striving different ways in my heart. I felt
no desire for anyone's company; that hunger
had ended at last; instead I kept on calling
on Jesus to come.' She paused, then pointed to a spot:
'Two days after, when I was standing there, just there,
I felt a great light come into my heart; my troubles
all left me and I was happy at last.'

I questioned her then from the catechism
as contained in the Book of Common Prayer, in the Form
of Baptism for those of Maturer Years.
Her answers being sound, I requested one of the company
to bring me water in a gourd from a pool.
Then, blessing it, I baptised the Hottentot leper,
Antje Rautenbach, in the name
of the ever-blessed, the glorious Trinity.

It was indeed a solemn time to my mind:
several things conspired to make it so:

190

First, the order of the sacrament, the great
enfranchising words; Second, the person baptised,
a leper woman nursing a light within her;
Third, the congregation, outcast lepers
of an outcast race; Fourth, the place, a scrub-grown
river frontier under a wintry sky.
Yet I, I felt that the angels of heaven were present
rejoicing over another heir to salvation;
that desolate place was the house of God,
the gate of heaven was in that place.

THE OLD MAN'S FIDDLE

Five people we stood round our goods on the sand,
the old man, my mother, John, Sarah and me:
'We've done with the smoke of the mills and the wars;
the blue sky looks healthy, the skyline is free.
now if you agree
just hand me my fiddle
and thank the good Lord
that we're shot of the sea.'
So we sang to his fiddle
my mother, John, Sarah and me,
my mother, John, Sarah and me.

Four people we knelt round the bed in the tent,
the old man, John, Sarah, and me.
'She's done with the coughing and spitting of blood
and crying all night for the old countaree.
Now if you agree
just hand me my fiddle
and thank the good Lord
that her soul is set free.'
So we sang to his fiddle
John, Sarah and me.

Three people we heard the tall officer's praise,
the old man, Sarah, and me.
'The jackals won't get him because of the stones
we packed on his grave by the river Bashee.'
'It's as it should be,
so hand me my fiddle
and thank the good Lord
for a fair memory.'
So we sang to his fiddle
Sarah and me,
Sarah and me.

Two people we stand by two graves in the grass,
the old man and me.
It's hard she should die giving birth to a son,
it's hard that the babe's in eternity.
'Did this have to be?
You take up my fiddle
and beg the good Lord
to have mercy on me.'
So I played on his fiddle
as sweet and soft as could be –
but no one was there with me.

I came from a-courting to find the house dark:
'My father, it's me.'
but he's deaf to my voice and the cries of the owls
and the sounds that drift indoors from over the sea.
And so, silently
I take up his fiddle
and ask the good Lord
to make music for me;
then head-high, I lift it
and crash it across my knee,
and crash it across my knee.

I stroll past the churchyard, my girl on my arm.
'My father, it's me.'
'You've chosen a fair one who's healthy and warm,
but what has your loving to do now with me?

By next Janu'ree
come with a new fiddle
and thank the good Lord
for a child that's to be;
and maybe we'll hear it,
your mother, John, Sarah and me,
your mother, John, Sarah and me.'

SINQUOS

One morning I was in Grahamstown, and had disposed of most of my
stock, except for some fat slaughter cattle … I had a Gaika Kafir,
Sinquos by name, in my employ for some time. He came to my tent in
the morning before daylight, and said he wished to speak to me. I got
up, and followed him a short distance from the wagons. He then told me
that he must go to Kafirland, as he was called by his captain. I tried to
persuade him not to go; but in vain. Then I said to him, 'Sinquos, what
must I do with your cow and heifer calf?' He answered, 'If I come out
again I know you will give them to me; but if not, give them to your son
John.' 'Am I to understand then that there will be war?' I rejoined. But
he did not confirm my suspicion otherwise than by advising me to
inspan as quickly as possible, and not to stop before I was over the
Fish-river Rand …
        (From *The Kafir War of 1836* by John Montgomery)

Inkoos! Wake up! wake up, Inkoos!
The fire is lit, the oxen inspanned.
Begorrah, it's mad you are, Sinquos!
The dawn star shines on the dewy land.

Inkoos must say goodbye to me.
So you don't take to my company?

I must go back to Gaika's kraal.
Have I been hard on you at all?

Inkoos, no: but I must go.
The fire is lit, the oxen inspanned.

And what if I should now say no?
The dawn star shines on the dewy land.

My Captain he called me in the night.
Does he plan to set the land alight?
The dawn star shines on the dewy land.

My Captain he called, and I must go.
The fire is lit, the oxen inspanned.
Will there be war? Say Yes or No?

Inkoos, trek now, trek over the river!
Your cow and your calf, do I keep them forever?
The dawn star shines on the dewy land.

Till I come back, keep them, Inkoos.
The fire is lit, the oxen inspanned.
And if you don't come back, Sinquos?

Then give them both to kleinbaas Jack,
the fire is lit, the oxen inspanned.
He never came back, he never came back.
The dawn star shines on the dewy land.

BLIND UNCLE STEVE

'Now who rides here,' Blind Steven cries,
'Across the wintry land?'
'It's our son's girl with long hair flying
and a letter in her hand.'

'What says the letter will happen now
Hermanus the chief has died?'
'Mounted men by threes and fours
will harry the countryside.'

'Just as I turned from the Beaufort road
a redcoat corporal cried:
Tell them their son'll be home tonight,
and say they have cause for pride.'

Blind Uncle Steven's head is cocked
like a watch dog's, on one side.
'Be careful of rumours in time of war –
what if the redcoat lied?'

Aunt Sal's eyes flashed and she turns to the girl.
'Your uncle's wits are wild.
Why should the redcoat lie to you?
Come sit by the fire, Child.'

Blind Uncle Steven speaks right on:
'If the redcoat's tale be true
why do I hear five sets of hooves?
Have four come out of the blue?'

Aunt Sal cries out: 'Now stop such talk.
My eyes are strong and clear
and I can see but one man riding
against the skyline there.'

But Uncle Steven does not stop:
'One set of hooves beats still;
I guess the four are hidden close
in the thorns at the foot of our hill.'

The women watched the rider come
all down the hill and out of sight.
Then four shots crash and echo far
into the cold twilight.

Old Steven cries: 'Sal, stop sobbing.
One horse is coming, galloping wild.
Don't rush to the stable door, my dear.
The saddle is empty, Child.'

THOMAS PHILIPPS'S PICNIC, 1821

See *Thomas Philipps, 1820 Settler*, ed. Arthur Keppel-Jones, pp.94-6.

The camp

Says Thomas Philipps to Doctor O'Flynn
on the first night out of a four-day jaunt,
'Since Mr Dalgairns and the younger men
have pitched our camp in so pleasant a haunt,
let us toast their healths in the very best wine.'
Which is done to our hearts' desire
by the light of a wild wood fire
in spite of
in spite of
the noises of jackals and river horses
and the tune
of the crickets, and, yes, of the moon,
and the sharp strange stars in their courses.

As rubicund as the very best wine,
and happily drifting down Lethe's dark stream,
our worthy but weary Doctor O'Flynn
is soon not sure where his homesick dream
and this African picnic end or begin.
All around his Elysian wherry
he is hearing the pipers of Kerry
and never
oh, never
the noises of jackals and river horses
and the tune
of the crickets, and, yes, of the moon,
and the sharp strange stars in their courses.

Says Mrs Dalgairns from a leopard skin
on a straw palliasse in the ladies' marquee,
'It's the strangest of beds I've ever been in.'
When the candle is snuffed, 'Oh, husband! Help me!'
(contralto) cries out dear Mrs O'Flynn.
In diaphanous bedtime attire

she appears 'mongst the men round the fire
all because of
all because of
the noises of jackals and river horses
and the tune
of the crickets, and, yes, of the moon,
and the sharp strange stars in their courses.

The ever-courteous Philipps approaches,
reassuring the ladies, 'No cause for alarm!
we'll defend you from all these nocturnal poachers!'
While Doctor O'Flynn leads his wife by the arm
to the feminine quarters, with muffled reproaches.
And we men return to our work
to hear the sweet pop of each cork
clearly above
clearly above
the noises of jackals and river horses
and the tune
of the crickets, and, yes, of the moon
and the sharp strange stars in their courses.

'It is three o' the clock on a moonlit night!
All's well!' we yodel with long-drawn halloos,
with resonant voices, with fiddle and flute,
we surprise the old echoes with musical news –
till we sink, and we snore, in the rising light.
We are dozing here in the sun
long after the birds and the dawn
have silenced
have silenced
the noises of jackals and river horses
and the tune
of the crickets, and, yes, of the moon
and the sharp strange stars in their courses.

THE DANCE

You girls, come dressed in Regency style –
what if a year out of date?
See Edward Philipps, that glass of fashion,
flashes a confident smile
from under an oribi hat;
and many a dandy eager fellow,
quite ready to fall to the tender passion,
steps forward in veldschoens, turmeric yellow.

Oh, dance all night round the wild wood fire
to tunes from Vienna and Wales,
and forget, in the sway of your heads and your spines,
in the rising beat of desire,
just how uncouth are these vales;
to the magic of fiddles your feet
trace Druid circles and Saxon lines
'twixt fever trees and fluitjiesriet.

From over the river among high rocks
young Xoxo and Nomsa stare.
Who are these dancing around the fire?
abafaz' are the skirts and the flowing locks,
amadod' are legs and short hair.
And under those beautiful clothes
are their bodies like ours stung by desire?
Abafaz' the belles, amadod' the beaux,
amadod' abafaz', the beaux and the belles.

HOW TO REMEMBER OUR ANCESTORS

I

It is festival time in the monument.
Next to the fountain bubbling in the foyer
one of a bunch of flowering girls

throws her head back and laughs, and laughs,
incredulous at something someone has done or said
she shakes the red shock of her hair
into a burst of flame.

Uncle Tom Bowker, you ought to be here.

II

In the nineteen fifties a gentleman from Johannesburg,
from the world of the silver screen
decided to make a 'frontier epic'
vivid with authentic experience.
Were there still a few old stagers about
who'd been lads in 1879?
Tom Bowker, M P for Albany, said,
'Let's see what we can do.'

They did the rounds of Upper and Lower Albany,
but all the likelies
seemed to have died since Uncle Tom
shook hands with them last at the Bathurst Show,
– except old Isaac – What's-his-name –
Bradfield? Timm? Tarr? Emslie, or Long?
Anyway, there they sat, in the Pig & Whistle, Bathurst,
a living Settler Monument
in regular use since 1830.
'Uncle Isaac,' said Uncle Tom,
'tell this gentleman from Johannesburg
how you were ambushed down at Watersmeet.'

'Ambush? Watersmeet? Let me see now …'
His pondering pause was filled
with doves and kokkewiets.
'Yes. Four of you on horses:
you, and Tarr, and Bradfield,
and maybe a Timm or a Purdon.'

'Which Timm? Which Tarr? Which Bradfield?
Man, my life's been full of them.

'Well, you said you were courting the sister
of one of them at the time.'

'Was I now? Well most men had sisters then;
those days, families was large. And I,
well, I did quite a bit of courting in those days.
What was this girl's name?'

'I don't know. But I do remember
one thing you said:
Her hair was a lovely red.'

'Red hair?'

'Yes.'

There was a long, long second of bird-haunted silence
as two pairs of old blue eyes
exchanged the secret of their delight.

Then Uncle Tom, pulling himself
back into history, swallowed and said:
'Yes, you and her brother and the others
were riding down to the drift
and just when you reached the crossing at Watersmeet
it happened. Tell this gentleman what happened.'

'Of course! I remember now –
what a beauty she was! Her name?
Wait now, let's see, it'll come, it'll come …'

'Well, you and her brother …'

'Did she have a brother? Likely enough.
Most girls had brothers those days;
families was large.'

'You and her brother,' said Uncle Tom.

'Now, what was her name! But oh,
what a peach of a girl!'

The better to remember, Uncle Isaac rose
and walked to the open window, and stared
into a blue bright sky
alive with unsolicited song.

Uncle Tom turned to the gentleman and said
'His memory's not what it was two years ago.'

And the man from the world of the silver screen
was moved to say:
'Who wants to be bothered about an ambush
when his mind's ablaze again
with a red-headed peach of a girl?'

FOR A THEATRE FOYER
The Nico Malan Theatre, Cape Town

To hear the changing language of man's heart
to watch his passions move on dancing feet
delighted both by instinct and by art
within these walls our thinking bodies meet

ANYWHERE

My life half-spent, I'd left the savage wood
for an ancient path across the bare plateau,
but unmarked side-tracks grew until a low
bind-weed of doubt ensnared me where I stood.

I stood where three roads met; and as I turned
quick eyes from each to each my terror grew.
Then lightning cracked the sky to chasms, through
which squalls of twisting sleet and thunder churned.

And when at last the pools gleamed still, a jet-
black thorn, which in the gale I'd taken
for old Lear's cursing ghost, now stood unshaken
by wind or ague, where those three roads met.

Slow-moving speck the unknown traveller grew
to hero's height; before I could, he spoke,
turned angry, raised his staff and, whirling, struck
his shadow; stared; with nonchalance withdrew.

And then another, slow, in silhouette
a pale-robed beggar blind along the road
by which I'd come. The stick-tap stopped; he stood
beside that twisted thorn where those roads met.

Some far wind-fury tore the sagging skies;
from the flaming west a lurid light, in flood
across the high plateau, picked up a blood-
stained fist round staff, and great, sightless marbled eyes.

Arms spreadeagled, through bearded mouth he cried:
'My father, Laius, is this the fatal place?'
The yawning space that settled round that voice
pressed on us both till both were petrified.

I dreamt: although my body could not move
soft voices came and told how grief was gone.
Gentle and proud between bent thorn, blind stone
two girls consoled that crossroads with their love.

No tree nor stone confronts me when I wake:
three unmarked roads, the plain as ever bare.
With ease I make my choice in the dawn-grey air.
The road I dreamt that those four took I take.

South Africa 1976–1989
Songs and Ballads

Grahamstown

'BODY GROWS OLD, HEART STAYS YOUNG'
Guga mzimba, sal' inhliziyo

I

Before we troubled
the Cape of Storms
or shook the Highveld
with horses and arms,
before the births
of Shaka, Retief,
old Zulus were chanting
this joy-in-grief:
'Body grows old,
heart stays young.'
Such was the heart's-ease
in their song.

II

Now, as we drive
or are driven apart
till none dare give
of the love in his heart,
as bodies grow chill
as spears to each other
and clouds drift still
through ominous weather,
'Hearts grow old
in bodies yet young,'
runs like a shudder
through our song.

III

In ages of iron
gilded with gold
the Cross and Orion
swung high and cold.
Great Hunter, Great Lover,

swing low, shine warm
till our tongues recover
that ancient charm:
'Body grows old,
heart stays young'
again be the sequence
of all song.

HOMELAND HAIKU

Thin cattle lowing
over thorn kraals, chieftain's graves.
A herd's voice quavers.

The horns of new moons
come quicker than cattle come
for my lobola.

From birth boys have heard
old men's endless women's talk
of men who are gone.

White men's aeroplanes
bring bread-money from fathers,
black moles underground.

He who comes but once
a year to mother's hut does not
sweeten the season.

The headlights of cars
prowl and roar through moonless nights.
The lions are dead.

Her withered fingers
shake but she sets flame to dry
cowdung under pots.

His one blanket's red
turns brown, clings closer, colder
as the embers die.

SOWETO

In years of ease
we took Soweto for granted; but
through hurricane weeks like these
what should we do? Bang, bang shut
our doors, our hearts, clench our fists and faces?
In secret collapse on unaccustomed knees?
or let a wild scream from the gut
climb the concrete of our public places?

Everywhere
terrifying silence or terrible noise;
smoke of schools in the air;
determined, in secret, once footloose boys,
successfully through their apprentice paces,
make more petrol bombs to fling at our fear.
Our hierarchy publicly keeps its poise.
a tired cop tightens his loose bootlaces.

Somewhere
a party's in congress; someone declares
there is no crisis here.
Though B P C or SASO, it is said,
are stirring up trouble between our races,
there's no real injustice nor cause for fear;
though there may be some drop in stocks and shares,
the Pentagon needs our minerals and bases.

Nowhere
escape; still safe in my skin I turn
to sniff, like a thin stray dog, the air.
Where, where today do the schoolrooms burn?
While deeper than all fear
I stumble through no-man's-land, through buffer spaces
hoping at last to reach and learn
the ground beneath all feet, all fists, all voices.

In hours like these
let's take no child for granted; let's curse

those treacherous years; grasp at, seize
each small chance for good, tenderly nurse
each just seed, rejoice in smallest traces
of mercy; open our heart, hand, door and purse.
Dear Law-makers, dear Law-breakers, may it please
the Gods to give us the needful insights and graces.

LISBON: 15TH-CENTURY BARCAROLE

Hours I listen and watch
you singing at rigging and hatch,
I die for love.

White sails belly; you turn
your eyes to the prow, not astern.
I die for love.

On the desolate quays I wait
early and late, so late.
I die for love.

Below or upon what rim
does your hull rot or skim?
I die for love.

Bare skyline strikes me blind.
Singing, you haunt my mind.
I die for love.

Silent, through ebb and through flood,
your keepsake burns in my blood.
I die for love.

Gain the whole world, if you must,
but when will you reckon the cost?
I die for love.

These poems were written for a cantata to be sung on a festive occasion. As the performance of miracle plays on board ship was common practice in the fifteenth and sixteenth centuries, I imagined the feast of the Epiphany being celebrated on the flagship of Da Gama's small fleet (the *São Rafael*, the *São Gabriel* and the *Berrio*) during the Christmas season, 1497, when Natal was given its name. In medieval times the three kings were given the names I use and allocated to the three continents; from which three continents the present population of Natal comes.

NATAL, 1497

I

Past shores no eye has seen,
beneath uncharted stars,
our three prows turn north-east;
the breeze sings high and keen.
On tilting decks from Portugal – *São Rafael*,
we'll hold our feast to India – *São Gabriel*,
on Christmas Day off Africa – *Il Berrio*.

On the flagship all's astir,
beneath our Captain's eye
we'll play the ancient play:
three wizards and a star.
From Macedon comes Melchior – *São Rafael*,
from India comes Casparo – *São Gabriel*,
from Africa comes Balthazar – *Il Berrio*.

In silence, by each keel,
the age-old knots are cut;
the gifted kings of earth
meet on our deck, and kneel.
From Macedon comes Melchior – with heavy gold,
from India comes Casparo – with frankincense,
from Africa comes Balthazar – with bitter myrrh.

II

Melchior, King of Macedon

The fateful star burns fixed above a ruined stable.
Is this the cosmic concord our philosophers foresaw?
How kneel upon these cobbles, bow to Hebrew peasants,
how leave my gold among these animals and straw?

                                    Chair' O Pammagiste.

Yet why should I now recall how the woman of Mantinea,
Diotima of mysteries, replied to Socrates:
'Great love is always poor, rough-skinned and weatherbeaten,
And couches out of doors with those of low degree.'

                                    Chair' O Pammagiste.

I kneel within the centre of my burning question:
can this poor swaddled thing among the colts and calves
be that half god, half man, nor mortal, nor immortal,
who saves the universe from falling into halves?

                                    Chair' O Pammagiste.

III

Casparo, King of India

'Whenever virtue fails
and lawlessness arises
there do I bring myself
to powerful incarnation.'

Recalling Krishna's words
to the trembling charioteer,
when all the signs were dark,
incense I bring, and prayer.

O may your house, dear Prince, be peace,
and not walled in on every side.
and may the windows be large and open
that changing airs from all the oceans
may move through quiet rooms.

209

Chorus   Shantih, shantih, shantih

May you be cooled and fed by them,
and not dismayed, nor blown about.
May none of your followers try to capture
your house for a restless inn or a prison;
O may your house be peace.

                                            Shantih, shantih, shantih

IV

Balthazar, King of Africa

O boy with the oxen
you ask a hard riddle
far darker than battle
that none here can answer.
Our prophets hear thunder –
a terrible river –
they say you will cross it;
they stay in the mountains.
We know when you've crossed it,
we know that your mother
will wash from your body
red mud of that river.
We pray that all peoples
will bind up your spear wounds,
and so we have brought you
this myrrh, my small master.

Chorus   Bayete, bayete,
                                            bayete, bayete

MAGNIFICAT

Mary: Our God who kept his word with Noah at the Flood
remembers his mercy this day.
This day his promises to Abraham our Father
bear fruit and are fulfilled.
His mercy is large as the ocean;

Kings: the humble and meek shall know it.
Mary: His justice like storms from heaven;
Kings: the mighty and rich shall know it.
Mary: The Lord of all creation keeps
Kings: his promises with men.
Mary: Hosannah, hosannah, hosannah.
                    Melchior: Chair' O Pammagiste.
                    Mary: Hosannah, hosannah, hosannah.
                    Casparo: Shantih, shantih, shantih.
                    Mary: Hosannah, hosannah, hosannah.
                    Balthazar: Bayete, bayete, bayete.
                    All: Hosannah, hosannah, hosannah.

WATCHING THE SEED-GRASS

Between our eyes and the racing clouds
the wind shakes the seed-grass to and fro.
We kiss, embrace; we all but forget
the crags, the black stream plummeting
the riven gorge below.

The grass-wind skims the disc of the sun,
it ducks and drakes through scudding sky.
Though light flows in and out of our faces,
and cool then warm waves soak our skin,
unchanged lie you and I.

Though this ephemeral flowing together
mean months, mean years in the gorge below
where frozen birds fall from the trees
beside dark pools, we'll not forget
the seed-grass shaking so.

Time for a moment is wrecked on these hills;
we lie eternal, in shade, in sun;
this place is nowhere, everywhere;
and our love, O my Love, is it ours only
or the dream of everyone?

THREE GLANCES AT ONE PHOTOGRAPH

I

Cause of a feigned regret, a lying laugh,
bright, unlucky as a peacock feather,
the flat reflection of this photograph
records dead seconds out of years together,
seems now a cold, a cryptic epitaph
for those who breathed in that delightful weather.

II

A message through the eye, the shock
of static moments moulded out of rock,
all shadows halted, death in the midday clock;
your hands curled like a frosted frond,
dark eyes focused on an earth beyond
the naked trees, reeds frozen in the pond.

III

Unasked for, unexpected, avoiding heart and eye
a presence returns to brush my lips and side,
the first wind of spring, shaking the naked branches,
my tired body quivers with the ghost of its bride –
a casual flash of phosphor on a single breaker
announcing whole oceans thronging in to tide.

TO AN AGEING FRIEND, AFTER HER DIVORCE

Now it's over
and you must break
with unringed hands that jerk and shiver
the still green bonds of many suns and rains,
find you never
another lover

whose early vision, growing weak,
transformed your garlands into chains.

Sure this must be,
at least for one,
an unpredictable break in the weather,
the far princess brought possibly near;
if he can see
how rain and sun,
how living, and dying, and being together
are rings to one tree – be kind to him, dear.

THE END OF AN AFFAIR

No! I'm not tired. Yes! I could cry
could howl to call our old love back again.
While you, so cool, concede you'll not deny
a few regrets, perhaps a twinge of pain.
Enraged by your patient apathy
I stare through the curtains at the sun-struck sea,
knowing you will smile a dead smile
should I suggest we stride, mile after mile,
hand in hand,
along the silver-wet, long, shuddering sand,
my suddenly distant love.

It's come to this? Swop full for empty heart,
divide the loaded keepsakes? They'll soon be
quite clean of past occasions, need not start
a single memory from you, or me?
As if to say, 'Remember etiquette,'
you offer me a casual cigarette;
as if to say, 'You know the milk is spilt;
why cry, why make it all so difficult?'
Across the table
you're far, withdrawn, in some disastrous fable,
my suddenly distant love.

It's dead you are; you do not hate, can't feel;
I know you ought; in anguish I ask why
there comes no flash, no flick of sunlit steel
through the cool, the unstirred curtain of your eye.
Instead, 'We'll soon forget' is all you say.
The tired waitress clears the things away.
How noon turned cold one hot day one December
and froze your eyes, I shall, I shall remember;
and how my rage
beat out itself in words on this dead page
and not on you, my love,
my suddenly distant love.

IAGO'S HANDKERCHIEF SONG

For the spider and the scorpion
love's but a little span;
after coitus the young bride
makes a meal of her man.

With us the process differs now;
Emelia shows more taste;
she lingers, gnawing me for years –
there's no unseemly haste.

But 'twixt this fair Venetian bitch
and my black boss, the Moor,
love shines divine, eternal,
and shows me hideous, poor.

Shall I endure this rank demotion?
From this fine wisp of cloth,
I'll spin my web; I'll catch, I'll sting,
then banquet on them both.

214

HAVING SEEN THROUGH THE PATHETIC FALLACY

No cord ties us to earth.
Our bloods are in different groups.
Remotely different seasons
set our ungovernable moods.

This southern seasonal swing
has four times come and gone
since last a living thing
burst from my chrysalis;

since the larger silk cocoon
of the Christian scheme was torn
and the cosmic hoar-frost stung
my soft heart into stone.

Neither North nor South
can warm a paralysis;
nor ritual, nor routine
change seasons such as this.

Keep the eye clear of despair,
unclouded by dreams or hopes.
No cord ties us to earth.
Our bloods are in different groups.

EPITAPH

He strove, both in and out of season,
to use his modest gift aright;
still went on rhyming without reason
far into the night;
rhymes of the desperate word,
absurd
as the flounderings of a beheaded bird.

He hammered for help on the doors of the sky,
he heard the dead silence of God;
lost in the syntax of how and why
to and fro he trod.
At last he halted, numb,
struck dumb
by his long suspended sentence to the tomb.

POST MORTEM

There's still some growth,
someone said,
in the nails and the hair
of the recently dead.

Once he'd observed
in a specimen room
an uprooted aloe
come into bloom.

LAZARUS

'Lazarus, by what way
does the Shepherd lead our stray
meanings to where they belong?
Lazarus, once-lost friend,
save me from this dead-end,
this death of communal song.'

'Mary was wild, and wailed,
distraught, Martha failed
to do the chores of the day;
and the Friend, en route to the cross,
at first seemed at a loss
just what to do or say.

216

'He stared and stared at the stone
beyond which flesh and bone
already stinking lay.
He grieved for all, he wept;
he lied, he said I slept.
They rolled the stone away –

'Then with authority,
he flung the choice at me:
"Lazarus, come forth!"
To one who once has heard
and risen to such a word
just what are poems worth?'

FLESH AND BONE

Though hungry human flesh,
condemned, alone,
may cry out like an animal,
that cry is lyrical and fresh
beside our metaphysical
arpeggios of bone.

Flesh can redeem, atone
for the human brute
by making itself a dance from its passion;
but bone for the soul must be broken, bone
be bleached, then patiently filed to fashion
our delicate, piercing flute.

Perhaps when the last days darken
proud flesh, pure bone
will rise to dance and play together;
the hosts of heaven will stare, will hearken,
while in the immaculate, heavenly weather
The Father smiles on the Son.

AN ODD THOUGHT

I have come to this lonely cliff
to listen and stare, to be free
of weariness, fever and fret.

Below in a sunny cove
a couple of bathers quarrel
while their transistor set
drowns the ocean in cries
of anguished insatiable love.

A six-inch lizard darts,
then stops on a flint left here
by a strandloper long since dead.
He cocks an eye at me.
An odd thought darts through my head:

This little quick-eyed lizard
who lives here close to the waves
knows just what he needs, he is free;
we people, self-possessed,
are our very own runaway slaves.

POINT OF VIEW

Viewed from this height
the shadow of that pine
is stronger than the tree.

Its shadow is solid, flat,
black on the fine green parchment
of the ephemeral grass.

The tree itself seems frail,
so three-dimensional,
a stage prop of shredded paper.

218

Who, carelessly seeing
that clear shadow only
is able to reconstruct

so frail, so delicate a thing?
Before the rising or setting
of the one-eyed sun

the tree is all its own,
sieves the morning air,
gropes at the moon by night

or fixes itself to the earth
by taking sidereal shots
at countless points of light.

Look for, find the tree.
Clarity's a trick
of a dictatorial sun.

How often I mistake
firm, flat shadows for
substantial air-filled things.

WHOEVER-WHATEVER-YOU-ARE

Come.
The hour is yours,
the invitation open and urgent.
Come.

With whom am I pleading?
I do not know,
but, Whoever-whatever-you-are,
come, come.

Perhaps you think I am merely
a forbidding penal island on which

old flames and infantile fears
mutter treason, or madness –
if I were to set them free
what would I do, what would I be?

My long-term inmates are blind
to what you will discover in me:
new branches in bud, white flowers waiting
the hawk-moth's trembling tongue;
long lakes, blue gorges through granite,
seed-grass pulsing on gentle hills
which no one has ever looked upon.

Come, new eyes,
take nothing for granted,
expect nothing startling or familiar,
be equally open to boredom or surprise,
but come.

Beyond the frontiers of my skin
a continent of naked tribes, strange beasts,
sources of hidden rivers.
I know it is there, but how can I explore it?
How can we draw ourselves out of ourselves?
We can only be willing to be drawn.
I have been willing a long time now.
Come.

Perhaps you will not come until
I set my captives free.

Whoever-whatever-you-are,
you who alone can make
me known to me.

I open the gates
I let them go.

They take a long time to quit their cells.

I do not like the way some look at me;

I like it less when they don't even look behind.

And still you do not come.
Perhaps when my only care
is no longer my own long deep
solitary confinement,
when I long to know what has become of them,
perhaps,
Whoever-whatever-you-are,
perhaps you will come.

Pilgrimage to Dias Cross
A Narrative Poem

Illustration by Cecil Skotnes

PILGRIMAGE TO DIAS CROSS
A Narrative Poem

Prologue

Angered by the political exploitation of differences between the peoples of his country, the ageing speaker makes an imaginary pilgrimage to a favourite spot: Kwaai Hoek, or 'False Island', the headland off the southern African coast where Dias raised a cross five centuries ago. On his way he is joined by historical ghosts who haunt the immediate hinterland. Between sunset and midnight the pilgrims cross the no-man's-land of sand dunes which connects the headland to Africa. They make a fire from flotsam, and keep vigil there, until the spirit of Dias appears. His presence enables them to affirm their common humanity and to share their songs, which transcend their divisive histories.

This poem is embedded in the following historical and geographical circumstances.

On 12 March 1488, the Portuguese discoverer, Bartolomeu Dias, planted a padrão, or stone pillar surmounted by a cross, on a small headland, subsequently known as Kwaai Hoek ('Vicious Corner') on the Eastern Cape coast, between the mouths of the Bushman's and Boknes rivers. He had established that the African coastline did not continue south forever, but his mutinous crews made farther exploration impossible. His voyage heralded the closer linking of Europe, Africa and Asia.

Within a radius of twenty kilometres as the crow flies from Dias Cross are other historical sites of symbolical significance.

Sixteen kilometres to the east, and about five inland, lie the ruins of Theopolis – the Hottentot (Khoikhoi) mission station, founded by the London Missionary Society in 1814. One of the leaders of the community was Cobus Boesak, a great elephant hunter, whose intervention in the battle of Grahamstown (1819) was decisive.

Twenty kilometres to the north, overlooking the Bushman's River valley, is the farm 'Belton' or 'Raven Hill', the site of Wait's Party of 1820 Settlers. Among this group was the youthful Jeremiah Goldswain, whose *Chronicle* is one of the most vivid, amusing and moving accounts we have of the settler struggle for survival on the frontier.

To the west, lie three places of interest.

First, at a distance of about twenty kilometres, and close to the town of Alexandria, lies the farm 'Melkhoutboom', once owned by Karel Landman, a frontiersman who, late in the Great Trek in 1837, led a group of Dutch farmers into Natal.

Second, at a distance of thirteen kilometres, isolated in a large field variously planted with oats and lucerne, stands a small clump of indigenous bush. On the edge of this lies the grave of Nongqawuse, the Xhosa prophetess who with her uncle the diviner Umhlakaza instigated the Cattle Killing of 1856, which resulted in the so-called national suicide of the Xhosa.

Third, about six kilometres from Dias Cross lies the farm 'Richmond'. Here James Butler (my grandfather), a young consumptive from London, stayed as the guest of the Shaws in 1877 during the Seventh Frontier War. He later moved to the Karoo, where he recovered his health, married the grand-daughter of an 1820 Settler, produced seven children, and ran a newspaper and a bookshop. His liberal and pacifist thinking was not popular. His funeral in 1923 was attended by members of all races.

The use of the word pilgrimage may puzzle some. The destination of the journey in the poem is not a holy shrine in the accepted sense of the word; nor are the pilgrims typical. (We are ten thousand kilometres and almost six hundred years from Chaucer's Canterbury pilgrims.) But a pilgrimage of any restless mind to its own historical shrines may serve similar liberating and creative purposes.

(See notes on p. 268.)

I

Lightning flickers in sheets across our frontiers;
raucous atmospherics laugh at the lies in our news.

I switch off, angry, ashamed. I think it better to roam
where breakers totter and crumble late in the afternoon.

There I can howl like a dog, or falling to my knees
invoke the wrath of God on racial idolatries.

How many must die each day, choked like Laocoön,
lassoed by this devious dream, whose coils roll on, and on?

Cry! What shall I cry? Shall I call up the restless dead
to purge our days of the nightmare these politicos have made?

How can an ageing man with glimmerings of belief
get rid of his futile fury, his embitterment of grief?

Hoping against all hope, raging against my rage,
I take a deep breath, and laugh. I shall go on pilgrimage.

II

On the highest coastal hill
in a gap in the shaken trees, I pause;
shadow-blotched, still as a stone-age man, I stare.
A dazzle of sands
staggers into the far white froth of the sea;
sea receding south into the arctic ice,
sweeping east to India,
west to the Americas,
but here to the north it beats
this blunt butt-end of Africa:
beaches, cliffs, dunes and coastal scrub,
this mini-desert of sand.

Far, on its seaward fringe
the focus of my eye:
a lonely wreckage of rocks
half-in, half-out of the endless thud
and sliding hiss of the tides;
a bonewhite cranium crowned with scrub
dark and evergreen.

Sea encountering sand, rock encountering sea,
and sea and land all round encountering the sky;
unbroken its encirclement, it rises
doming round and over those far rocks and me.

No sound except
the interminable
pounding of the sea.

III

Five hundred years have come, have gone:
the giant light of day,
starry hosts by night,
the changeful moon,
her slavish train of tides,
wind, sea spray, rain,
rubbing to erase

one slight signature written in stone by Dias,
there, with a mutinous crew.

He did not guess
what destinies of consciousness,
fleets, empires, tribes, tongues, gods
hung in his rotten rigging, spun
in the salt white sand that filled the space
between the cross's square-cut base
and the ill-fitting socket built
of the bonewhite, soft
indigenous stone.

It marked a limit
to failure and success;
far enough to change the charts
of all ships since.

Why should he listen,
or look inland, beyond the bluff?
His business was the still unsullied sea.

But mine? To finger unstrung beads and flints,
potsherds from stone-age middens among these dunes?
blue-and-white china chips, spent musket-balls
from sites of abandoned settlements?
to mutter and to stutter land-locked questions,
ventriloquising voices from the shore?

IV

Between the dark scrub and the moonwhite stones –
deserted site proposed for the City of God –
I hear a murmur of birds, a scraping of twigs
washed by rippling voices quickened by clicks.

Boesak returns to base with twenty tusks.
He hears his children's voices invading the hot
amorphous day, intoning the alphabet,
reciting tables, and then the ten
commandments gentled in plangent hymns,
white justice blind to darkness of skin.

At dusk his hands, like outsize leaves, hang slack
drooping from wrists, balanced on his knees.

Suddenly ten fingers spread
transfigured starfish swimming in flame.
Behind them, barely seen, the cave of his mouth
emits sad echoes of ancient song:

Honey-skinned as apricots
we shone when summer thunderstorms
caught us on the move
from spring to spring.

By moon we sang when clan
met clan at waterholes for weddings, so danced,
so lightfoot on the soil
we never wound.

Our bows lay idle in the shade.
We passed from singing lip to lip
the fire-hardened bowl
of honey beer.

The fire-hardened bowl is broken.
No shard is large enough to scoop
a mouthful of water or carry
a fire coal

Brandy and smallpox burnt our flesh;
on shrinking plains our numbers shrank;
once Men-of-men, we dwindled into middlemen,
now with the Blacks, now with the Whites,
settling the prices of tusks, horses and guns.

When Colonel Willshire saw Makandla's men
snapping their spearshafts off upon their knees,
in vain he cried for his Dragoons, in vain.

Then it was that I, last of the great Khoi chiefs,
with my hundred and thirty buffalo hunters
mounted on trotting oxen, crested the hill.

We took in the sight. Where to throw our weight?
Or to lounge in the shade, take snuff, and smile,

watching those tribes who'd eaten all our honeycomb
eat each other up?

I gave my commands.

Down we came in open order,
crack shots to a man,
and took them in the flank.
We picked off the chief men clad in leopard skins,
withdrew a little space, reloaded,
then down we came again. Again. Again.

Looking at my children, and their children,
I see that use of power was misplaced.
God grant that day again and we
will wipe out the English gunners
firing grape-shot from the flanks.

The fire-hardened bowl is broken.
No shard is big enough to scoop
a mouthful of water or carry
a fire coal.

Sweet hope soured, fermented, seethed;
many mutinies quickly broken.
Each sentence ends
with a jerking rope,
a rattle of musket fire
pocking the plastered barrack wall,
skull bones cold under fallen lintels.

No sound but the wind, no legend strummed
on a ghorra's humming string. In huts on farms,
poor houses in towns, descendants diet
on rotten fruits of defeat. Forgotten
Theopolis; forgotten also
O elephant slayer, O buffalo killer,
Boesak, Khoikhoi chief.

Still alive he stalks with me,
crossing the lengthening streaks of shadows
between me and Dias Cross.

V

Near raw ploughed earth on 'Raven Hill'
are angry voices; silences; we hear
in English dialect loud argument
surge and subside in the heat of desert wind.
Come, come, Mister Keen, I cannot raise your rations.
— Then what, Mister Wait, about our wages? — I pay
what the law permits. — You bastard, cries Jeremiah,
the children are crying for bread.

Through berg-wind weather for days and days,
their bare feet trudge. In jerky shade they ease
(using white mimosa thorns for spikes)
the fluid from each other's blistered feet.
Two hundred miles. A trial. Prison.
A year before some beggarly redress.

Fighting for bread and wages,
burning lime on the beach,
pivoting in the saw-pit,
courting Eliza Debnam,
riding supplies for the Army,
I had no time to question
my title to be here.

Half-starved in dear old England
we fell for the golden promise
of one hundred acres of land.
What did we know or care for its history?
Hunger doesn't ask such fancy questions.

And now?

In hiding from the Special Branch
a great-grandson prophesies
a new Makandla, Nelson Mandela.

After ninety days' detention
a girl in faded denims shouts again,
'Bread and justice for the Blacks!'

Her cousin in Anglo American
she calls a fascist pig.
Scorn and anger twist her mouth.

Pondering balance sheets
he smiles indulgently at Marx
and all simplistic radicals.

No radical but angry, another
self-exiled, cold in London,
burns his call-up papers.

'I shall never go into the Townships
to shoot down Blacks for the Nats.'
His brother's in the Parabats.

What is happening to my seed?
all choked by tares, all
fallen on stony ground?

He kicks a pebble from his path.

A trio of ghosts as the sun goes down.
A pale apocalyptic blaze
over the Outeniquas.

VI

At Melkhoutboom near Boknes River mouth
Karel Landman shouts, 'Trek! Trr-ek!'
A cry to curdle the sky. Above ten waiting wagons
a bamboo whipstock waves, the whiplash flickers,
licks air like a snake's tongue, cracks above the backs
of the first of sixteen pairs of bullocks to the span.
Long chains lift from the grass, wheel spokes turn,
wince under weight, their iron tyres cut
deep ruts into wet turf.
Beneath the new white tilt a bright child chatters.
'At last, at last!' Her mother stifles tears.
The endless hunt for her home's begun again
beyond philanthropy's manicured finger,

231

beyond the cattle-lifter's assegai,
beyond the imperial reach of British arms,
somewhere, a pastoral people's paradise.

Always this dream of possessing the land,
of being possessed by it. Land can grip
the spine of a people, like my people, or the Jews.
But where different peoples dream about
the same piece of earth, the dreams clash
and the frontiers darken and bleed.

There was time enough to brood: that winter trek
across the treeless plains; our daughters gathering
cow-dung for fires on pale blue mornings
in frost-white grass; those plains left empty
by Sekonyela's and by Matiwane's wars.

At last we reached the great escarpment's edge;
from there we gazed in silence; long we looked
into the threat and promise of Natal,
listened, so silent, and so long, I wished
some pious soul would snap the spell with a psalm,
to bless those awesome minutes. Instead, Rudolf,
my right-hand man, in his dead, flat, practical voice,
exclaimed, 'Woe! Woe awaits the land
with such dark shadows on its frontiers!'

Fugitives, we were sustained by a dream.
History, with a vengeance, has brought it all to pass:

She gave authority and strength to us
to draw the frontiers where we would. My sons
have drawn them, and their sons re-draw them still
on maps, with laws, new complex constitutions.
Now my grandsons govern nothing but a realm of shadows.
They dread by night that half a century
of power to impose their dream on other men –
dream of a divinely sanctioned love of one's own –
has left them loveless, loving themselves alone.

What is there left when the dream
ends with a desolate dusk?
The sky is vaster, lonelier

for the flight of four white egrets leaving
the homing cattle on the vlei.

VII

Like rolbos blown to a halt in a fence we stop
beside a copse of old, dark trees. A hole
in the ground, a mound of damp clods. Some Xhosa men
come stumbling into the streams of the wind
to a weird, slow dirge. They place in the pit
a shrivelled corpse in a worn kaross.
Women squat on the grave's edge; they keen and weep.

O Nongqawuse, O Nongqawuse! Girl,
gleaming wet you rose from the pool of Um Gxara.
You prophesied such victory for the Xhosa!

Don't harvest your crops! Kill, kill all your cattle!
Our mighty dead with numberless horns will rise,
chanting and lowing, from this river; Umlungu and Mfengu,
all will drown in the sea; old men and women
shall shed their wrinkles and smooth-skinned as I
shall welcome them all with singing and dancing.

From Kungwa's Kraal to Umhlakaza's Place
a rumour of bellowing cattle disturbs the grass.
Like thunderclouds that bring no rain the gloom
rolls on, and softer on, into the cricket chirr
and the whimpering cry of starving children,
on, and on, and into our day.

They do not die of hunger only, but under the guns
of the police, in the Kangaroo Courts, judged
by Comrades true and false. Their schools are shut
by foreign prophets, followers of Verwoerd and Marx.

Nongqawuse rose and stretched.
She took her long-stemmed beaded pipe
from old pursed lips and spat in polite contempt.
I, a prophetess, say this to all of them:
All prophets, without knowing it, are false;
we can't control the dreams we sprout:

233

men of power harvest them to thatch
big huts for themselves.
The prophet is left out of their dreams.
He ends his life in prison, on an island in the sea,
or withers in aged exile, as I did, here.
No chieftains, no herds of cattle
came out of my river of dreams.
Now – will it flow with blood again
leaving a driftwood of bones?
Young men are filled with visions,
they raise their fists, forward they dance,
they die with songs in their mouths –
songs I was so slow to learn,
Ntsikana's hymn from the Mankazana
and one from the mouth of Enoch Sontonga
completed by the great Mqhayi.

Men learn little. Each generation
in its own time must endure
whatever it is to be woman or man.

We turn our backs on the burial grove,
on the fading western light, and walk
away from the troubled earth and history
east, where a few stars glitter like mica dust
above a darkening sea.

VIII

Drawn by a candle-lit window at 'Richmond'
we all stare into a room. The light picks up
'James Butler' in black on a leather bag.
A very young man unpacks his letter book,
moves to the table, trims the candle.
Shoulders shaken by spasms of coughing,
he waits with patience, goose-quill poised.

'Dear folk in London, the froth from my lungs'–
No; far rather catch this African scene
in a legible web on the naked sheet:
register rainfall, record each season's

flowers and butterflies; farms inefficient
from lack of trained labour. Stick to the facts –
my nearness to God is anyone's guess.

Familiar dread of early death is calmed
attending to this unfamiliar world.
The cough's *memento mori* supervenes,
he drops his pen, pushes the pad aside.

There'll be no sleep for me tonight. Get up, walk,
under the early stars, familiarise
yourself with these new constellations,
sounds of night birds and insects,
scents of dew-wet coastal scrub,
mixed with the sounds and scents of the sea
and other emanations, more humane perhaps,
of this supposedly promising land.

Two weeks ago my best friend, Shaw, at night
returning from picket, was shot through the chest,
killed by accident, by one of his own men.
What do I know of the wars of this land?
At times I catch a clamour of ghostly voices
that haunt the minds of the men of this place –
English, High Dutch, Creole and Xhosa
and, sometimes, French and Portuguese.

As for the women – whatever will follow
my falling in love? What will befall
the children asleep in my aching loins?

Will this be the last of the Frontier Wars?
God, allow me to breathe.
I promise children who'll not submit
to the easy hatreds of the land.

IX

In the dark the plovers clatter and cry
above grass-covered dunes.
Owls and night-jars take over
as we pass through whispering scrub.

On the highest coastal hill
in a gap in the shaken trees, we pause.
There is no moon. Still as the dead we stare.

Then we plunge through slipping sands,
passing between dim gleaning dunes,
under a sky thick with the noise of the sea.

In no-man's-land
no man is himself,
histories are lost.

Voices – whose voices? –
heard, guessed at,
anonymous.

Before Xhosa or Boer I taught my sons
to fish off those loud rocks.
Gather what scraps of wood you cross.
Nights here are cold.

Nothing. The sound of breakers rising and falling.
I trip. I fall. I rise. I shoulder a branch
of a flotsam tree.

Footfalls sigh into rustling sand. I hear
a twig snap, the scrape of pebble on stone.
Each breaker swallows the other's dying roar.

Through dwarf wind-matted scrub the footpath
twists steeply up to the level top.
Cold and dark.

A chasm of silence
which all the falling breakers can never fill.
Nothing but the elements, sea, land, sky.

Often a journey ends on a height
and no one there.

X

Click of steel on flint.
A star struck into a fist full of grass.
Blow from pursed lips, gently blow.

Flame.

In the moment of spiritual need,
in the elemental cold,
feed the flame with the flotsam of history.
Splintered oarblade; rotten quiver;
smashed musket-stock; wormy wagon-spoke;
leg of a spindleback chair –
all serve as fuel as well
as driftwood brought down from inland
in summer's turmoil of waters.

All burn well,
flaking in flame,
layer by layer,
annual rings
peal from the pith;
each year's clear or twisted grain
unravels into ash.

Such deaths in flame
pull us out of the dark and cold.

Spokes round the fiery hub.
But where are the fellies, the rim?

XI

Midnight.
The blanket of silent air and stars
cannot console or still the restless surfaces.
On the eastern horizon
a paling of some stars, and then,
bit by bit, the moon: a white half-wafer,
mysterious in its incompleteness
mysteriously suspended over
the simmering chalice of the sea.

And there, beside his pillar of stone
the swarthy discoverer stands.

His truculent men who sweated to raise it,
tightening, easing ropes through palms,

are snoring long since.
Is his sleepless mind
still on the East, his Prince's hunger
for spices and converts? Or does he foresee
his cold homecoming, demotion
to third in command? About him cling
silent conspiracies. Records are lost.
The name of his ship? No soul knows.
Mere scraps of gossip, disguised facts.
On another voyage, Cabral in command,
in the deep Atlantic near Tristan da Cunha
in a sudden tornado's storm and noise
black waters will wolf him, ship and all.

We add what scraps of fuel are left,
feeding the flame. A sudden flare,
and he looks at us a long time, sitting there.

Ghosts of this coastline, he says at last,
for the first time I hear a pendulum swing
which I touched into motion
in passing, as it were. He smiles.
Your eyes all ask me,
what can I do for your tormented country?
And I reply,
What can you do for Portugal?

I have no words to meet your need.
May I share your circle of light
island of warmth in the cosmic cold?
Perhaps you will share my wine?
It has come a long way.
The vineyard is very old.

In silence the leather-bound flask is passed
from feathery hand to hand
completing the ring.

XII

All my people were weary and frightened
from the great seas and doldrums they'd endured,

distances, dead water in the casks, fresh
provisions long exhausted. In a great bay
we saw a rocky island whose lower slopes
were brown with sea lions, the upper white
shining with seabirds and centuries of dung.
There we erected a wooden cross
and called it Ilha da Cruz.
In its thin shade, among those beasts and birds,
we said mass. I called a council of my officers:
captains; pilots; sailing masters.
I made each swear to give his honest judgement.
All spoke with single voice: We must turn back.
I made them sign their names to that decision.

What can be said of the rest? I, Dias,
against their written resolve persuaded them
to go three further days with me.
But now, since my sole will
dragged each reluctant league
onto the naked chart,
I saw omens everywhere.

East of Ilha da Cruz
heavy surf betrayed a treacherous presence
of reefs and little islands. These, being low and flat,
I called the Ilheus Chaos. One of the crew
smirked at an unintended pun. I found
a passage safe enough – fifteen fathoms –
between them and the mainland.
East, beyond
the Ilheus Chaos, a promontory appeared
covered with small trees, bringing to mind a grove
of holm oaks. So I simply called it
Ponta do Carrascal. But once again,
the double meaning. Carrasco is a hangman.

Past Hangman's Headland I pushed on, and on,
against a mighty weight of tepid water
streaming from the north. Progress was laboursome.
Opposite a river mouth my time ran out.
João Infante, Captain of the Pantaleão,
put in for water; I gave that stream his name.

Who but one obtuse, after 'Chaos' and 'Carrascal',
would read 'Infante' as a man's name merely?
Something new perhaps had come to birth,
more powerful than any kingdom's son.

We turned round at the River of the Child.
My duty now? To set up sea marks,
signatures for our King.
Looking for prominent headlands,
the first we found on Saint Gregory's Day.
Here we erected the first of my stone padrãos,
here.

One of our belated chroniclers avers:
Dias drew away from that pillar
with pain and passion, as much as if
he'd left a son in exile there for ever:
remembering the peril to his person,
to all his men and ships; embittered that
their voyage should yield no other fruit
than a branchless little tree of marble planted,
its name soon lost on the charts. Later,
unlucky in its English translation,
another chronicle will call it
the pillory of Saint Gregory.
Kwaai Hoek, False Island
will not be the last of its names.

XIII

We know how the sounds of the air
and the roar of the sea
obliterate instinctive cries,
reasoning voices, prayers, curses, songs.
Over sea, sky, land,
the elements raise their arcane cries
which none can understand.
Among such acts and cries
we speak and act.

Sometimes a word outwits the cosmic noise,
sometimes by cunning or love
an action will flash into freedom,
feeling find form in song.

In the service of gods or systems
we forge our chains of command,
we submit and are bound by them.

They turn into scaling ladders;
we climb them, victors,
and fall through the rotten rungs.

All bloods and tongues
have rules for promotion, demotion,
elevations and losses of status.

Systems decay and die.
Where the Medes and the Persians?
Where the house of Aviz?

New patterns emerge.
In anger, duty, need,
we give ourselves to the weaving

and are woven into the web.
There is no escaping this.
Is this all there is for us ?

What single uniform
is fit enough for a man?
Can one garment gown a girl?

How long can we rest happy
in society's reach-me-downs,
a party's off-the-pegs ?

No culture is large enough to contain
the fullness of being of those who comprise it.
History's noise seems endless, like the sea's.

We are the traffic on its surface,
the life that sweats and labours,
the singing voices on the shore.

XIV

Each flings his voice against the sea's burden:
songs that haunt the heart and will not die
but ring like stricken bells, shiver with fire
each time new voices breathe through them; once more
from mortal mouths, from lips and throats
still fecund, not blasted or made barren by
the dread of labour pains, new-born amidst
the slow or sudden deaths of history.

When you come to a narrow mountain pass
wrap a small stone in grass
and cast it there, on Heisib's grave:
Heisib the often-defeated,
the often-buried, Heisib
the always-dying and laughing,
the never-quite-dead – O save us,
O Heisib, save your children,
on either side of the grave.

'Guide me, O thou great Redeemer,
pilgrim through this barren land;
I am weak, but thou art mighty,
hold me with thy powerful hand.

'If I take the wings of the morning: and remain
in the uttermost parts of the sea; even there also
shall thy hand lead me: and
thy right hand shall hold me.

'He who is our blanket of comfort,
the giver of life, ancient on high,
he is the Creator of the Heavens,
and the ever-burning stars.'

XV

I follow a ghost to the gleaming beach:
brown hands cupping a hole in his wind-skew beard,
with a toss of his pitch-black mane, he shouts,
You!

242

You are nowhere near your farthest east,
still have to double your Cape of Storms.
Speak! Hope for hearers!
Act! And pray for friends.
He swings a broad cold shoulder on to me.
Dawn light skids off his jerkin's hide
in sheets of ice.

Boat through the white surf bounces
to a mutinous caravel.

Sails unfold and fill.

XVI

The ghosts have gone to unquiet graves
but grasses and copses wet in the morning wind
are haunted by their hymns.

I raise my voice and sing with them
rejoicing, for once at one with all
in the fragile constitution of a verse.

It is a start at least.
Better a pilgrim's song when old,
one all-embracing dream,

than burn with rage
in a damned land
in an insolent age.

Sele! sele!
Ahom, ahom, ahom.

Family and Friends

Olive Schreiner's grave, Buffelskop

ODE TO DEAD FRIENDS
All Saints Day, South Africa 1987

(See notes on p. 272.)

Uys Krige (b. Swellendam 1910, d. Onrus 1987)
Sydney Clouts (b. Cape Town 1926, d. London 1982)
Monica Wilson (b. Lovedale 1908, d. Hogsback 1982)
Matthew Goniwe (b. Cradock 1947, assassinated near Port Elizabeth 1985)

Outside is no-man's-land.
Loud-hailers, cries, shots, then martial tunes;
black anger dancing, prancing out of hand,
snaffled by conscript boys in steel platoons.
Dear cloud of witnesses,
familiar with temptations to despair,
pour your reviving light through this distress,
on all whose pain no being seems to share.
Bright sun of many petals, burn
above us as we turn
our hearts' cold prisms to your warming rays,
to welcome them and spill in radiant line
such rainbows as define
each immemorial self unique in its design.

Uys is the first we meet.
Gifted with tongues; a cave of resonance;
declaiming French and Spanish down Long Street,
you brought Neruda into Afrikaans;
and still I hear you speak
to radical poets on their difficult art:
'Ideas will come; words won't, without technique.
Don't chase abstraction, write from your own raw heart.'
When asked to speak – for no more than an hour –
you smiled: 'But Madam, can you throttle
the Atlantic in a bottle?'
Artesian wit and prodigal of power,
they called you idler, jongleur, communist, clown.
Laughing, you tapped your frown,
'Three plays composed this month: I've just to write them down.'

Sydney's the next to come.
Lion, Devil, Table, mountains cut –
an exile's icons – on your London tomb.
But you are here, good friend, and laughing yet:
laughing at Metaphor,
at Metaphysic, at the ponderous men
who tell us what our maverick muse is for –
to parrot slogans for their regimen.
'Listen among the particles,' you said.
'Slake your being's thirst
where everything is first.
Seek out the pure, the singing fountainhead.'
Dead orthodoxies swarm with flies, but you
still prophesy the new
tradition of each day, the small shrubs bright with dew.

Under skies you love
you sleep; your regal mind, almost severe,
still moves with mountain winds over your groves
of breathing trees, then falls, and is everywhere.
While death encroached you still
sought to distinguish faces from their masks;
wise herbalist of secret shrubs that heal,
you touched with grace your final dying tasks.
Summoned as to a palace each new year
willing we came and always returned
aware of a heart that burned
with light and warmth, quite smokeless, ashless, clear.
Handing a heliochrysum sprig to me
you said: 'Those folk are free
who walk as though there's more to time than history.'

We were born in the same small town.
You wrote from jail, for help with English verse.
Bright boy, from grim Lingilihle, you had grown
to manhood while our tyranny grew worse.
Were freed; imprisoned; freed;
again you meet warm gatherings of friends;
are ambushed, tortured; after days found, dead;
and there, for Law and Order, your story ends.

But not for wife, child, brothers, comrades, these
for whom you are still magical.
We praise you! I recall
putting on Handel at news of your release.
You blew in on the wind. 'Look! I've arrived!'
nd round my room you jived
to the Hallelujah Chorus, laughing and alive.

We thank and praise you, friends:
forever Matthew, Monica, Sydney, Uys,
and countless more whose witness never ends
for us who struggle through this smouldering place.
Your intellectual light
still troubles minds that hate enlightenment;
your legacies of love still flood the sight,
still touch our hearts till some at least relent.
You pierce the smoke and darkness of our days.
Nothing is strange to you,
nor is this terror new.
Though steel-clad Caesar swaggers down our ways,
and crams his prisons with despair and night,
we still have second sight:
beyond the thronging darkness are people shining bright.

THE PLEIADES

My favourite stars are the modest Pleiades,
an indeterminate cluster of some said six,
some seven stars, they rightly refused to be numbered –

– new telescopes reveal they are numberless.
In all the folklore of the North these six
or seven are young, lovely, feminine.

Before I saw them I liked them for their sound,
the Pleiades. I learnt the stories about them,
these daughters of Atlas for the Greeks, in China

248

worshipped by girls as the sisters of industry.
They first appear in astronomical works
in the fifth millennium before the present time.

Egyptian temples were built to face their rising:
sacred to Athene, her immaculate Parthenon
welcomes them from the Acropolis.

***

Imagine my delight at finding them here
in the South, still a sacred centre of myths,
feminine as always, and women warm to them.

Theophilus Hahn tells us how the Khoikhoi
gather when they appear on the eastern horizon
dancing, singing, praying for food and rain,

while in the predawn dusklight mothers bear
their new born infants to an eminence
and teach them to stretch their hands to the friendly stars.

Among the Xhosa they're known as the isilimela,
derived from a word to dig, to plough, to put in seed,
announcing the birth of another year,

promising growth to plants and beasts and people,
not only the sprouting seed, but the coming out
of youths into the sunlight of manhood.

In the words of the great imbongi, S E K Mqhayi,
'We bind ourselves together with the Pleiades –
the stars we count our years by, the years of our manhood.'

***

Great Galileo's wise astronomers
using increasingly powerful telescopes
have changed the way we look at the skies, and measure
distances in years at the speed of light.

The stars can no longer be friendly. We are as lost
as ever we were with distances nearer home.
Sky measurements can teach us to question, to marvel –
but how to make friends? or how to be women, or men?

NTSIKANA'S BELL

I

In Cradock's location with my Quaker aunt
songs I heard with sounds from another world.
One got into my bones and still rings there.
'That', she said, 'is the bell song of Ntsikana.
His bell is a rock struck by a fist-sized stone.'

Making a frontier film the producer thought,
to be authentic, we should shoot a scene
in Xhosa country, something moving and strange.
I told them about Ntsikana, his burial, his bell.
'I've not been to Thatwa but we can ask the way.'

***

A desolate stretch of over-farmed smallholdings,
ill-kept shacks, dead motor cars, pigs, goats
and ragged people, many weaving their way
to a week-end of oblivion. No one
greeted us. One laughed aloud: Wrong area!

At last I found a school and the teacher's house.
He stood unsmiling in half his door. I asked,
'Which is the way to Ntsikana's grave?'
'Him! Your government gives that grave as a reason
to take our land and move us all from here.'
I said, 'I do not vote for Dr Verwoerd.'
'So?' He almost sneered. 'You, you English
settled us here.' I fumbled for a reply.
'A long while ago.' He shifted his eyes from me.

'Oh, yes, quite long enough for people's roots
to go down deep.' His bitterness shamed me dumb.

Nodding me aside, the producer asked
'Does this track lead to the Xhosa prophet's grave?'
A long, cold look. The slightest nod. 'Four miles,
in the bush, on the right.'
                    The grave? Ignorant,
I had expected a mound of uncut stones.
Instead, in ruin, a small brick shrine whose plaster
showed signs of mural pigment peeling off.
Time was flaying his favourite ox's hide.

The producer gave me a deprecating stare.
The camera crew did not undo their gear.

But there was still the bell; but which, oh which?
I stared at a dolerite mountain with aloes in bloom.
Which of those thousands of rocks would the bell stone be?
The crew were sulking, the villagers slouched away
or stood stock still, and stared. The silence was dead.

Then a slender Xhosa woman in her sixties
walked up and asked 'Intsimbi?' 'Yes,' I said.
She did not explain or point, she showed the way
at a pace that soon outstripped us all. Before
I saw her again I heard the bell, high F
and the C and the A below. To listen I paused,
watching my sweat drops blacken the purple stones.

The camera crew had not undone their gear.
No picture in that drab slab of dolerite.
True. But what of the woman, slender, elated
striking it in the right ancestral places
to make it ring and sing and echo among
thousands of other stones and aloes all
about those mountains under that sky?

I pleaded with the producer. 'Record the music!
Catch her hand as she strikes it out of the stone
then pan to the scene. Dub in a choir later.'

Silence. 'Get going chaps. Not much here.'
They turned their backs on the bell and stumbled off.

As for the bell-ringer, I offered her a note.
She'd expected no such thing. She'd volunteered
for Ntsikana's sake, and the joy of the bell.
Out of pure courtesy she smiled and took it.

No matter how often I cringe at my part in that day,
I've paid my respects to Ntsikana's grave,
I've heard his bell ring clear from the hand-struck heart of rock.

There is something about redemption itself in this;
part paid with the bitter blood-money of others,
part paid by gracious strangers, a gift outright.

II

When exiled Moses was tending sheep in the desert
God spoke to him through something a shepherd
would understand, a bush ablaze with life.

When Ntsikana went to look at his cattle
God spoke to him through a flash of the dawning sun
striking the side of Hulushe his favourite ox.

Strange things happened. Whirlwinds interrupted
his dancing. But he said nothing. Words must wait.
All day he stood at the gate of his cattle kraal.

His people wondered. They heard him softly humming,
humming a chant such as no one had ever heard.
Ele le le home, hom, hom —

a sound that came from an endless quietness,
deeper than the wells of words, above
the clouds where music breeds, *home, home —*

At last came the words themselves: not spoken, sung,
from the heart, an izibongo for Thixo,
using his own familiar Xhosa speech,

but stretched a little to let a new world in.
'Other poets give wonderful words to ponder.
So why', I ask, 'place Ntsikana first?'

Who else has his poems sung to his own tunes
nearly two hundred years beyond that day
death called for him? He showed his frightened people
how to dig his grave into that quietness.

SIGNAL HILL
After the fires that threatened the 1820 Monument

I

I am standing in ash alone on Signal Hill.
Still smouldering graffiti of burnt trees
are scrawled upon the huge wall of the sky.
Stripping the hill of its copse the fire has shown
these hand-packed stones, the signallers' old post.

When first I caught my breath at this wide view
it was nothing but a view. I have since written
a history of the refugees from Britain
who were settled between these hills and the sea;
and helped to raise a living monument
whose human roots first sprouted in this view.

A raging interior fire failed to stop
our annual festival, nor will this
succeed. A phoenix sings through flame and ash.

***

In nineteen thirty-seven
while the rest of campus
revelled in Rag
we slowly strolled up here
hardly daring, hoping
for mutual response.
Hailing from Johannesburg
when you saw this view

you cried with joy, 'The sea!'
You woke the same delight in me.

It was difficult to speak.
I ad-libbed with yarns
about features of the view
spun from trifles I knew
of lore or history.

A cold wind came up
with low cloud closing in
but neither was prepared
to be driven off this hill.

The only shelter seemed
a copse of tangled bush
but in its midst we found
the signallers' hand-packed stones.

Wrapped in our macs,
out of the wind
our bodies welcomed this wall.
The flame in each other
needed no kindling at all.

Almost sixty years.

Ignorant in our bliss
this was our first hearth,

the fire is burning still.

FROM THE SECOND BURIAL OF THOMAS PRINGLE

In 1970, as part of the celebrations to mark the 150th anniversary of the landing of the 1820 Settlers, the bones of Thomas Pringle, having been exhumed from Bun Hill Fields, London were re-interred in the Scottish Settlers' Memorial Church on the farm 'Eildon' the headquarters of the party of settlers which he led.

                   ... consider Pringle
a cripple since childhood. His parents thought
'It's Edinburgh and education for him,
he's fated to a sedentary life.'
He fell in love with the enlightened Muse.
The affair made small Scots impact but taught him enough,
in a different clime, to change that crutch into a wing
and sometimes a club.
                 A sedentary man
can organise a settler party, can
do all the dreary paper work, arrange
a three months' voyage, plan, apportion grants
of land, for two packed years take what part
a lame man might in pioneering work.

He talked to all, observed, he read, he wrote
but when his brother William arrived as head
he left the bookless frontier for the Cape;
a wild new world of images in his head,
sunlit distances, strange animals,
strange races, and wrongs done by all to each.

The radical Scots journalist soon got
into the hair of the Governor, Lord Charles,
a Beaufort, a being all but divine, who stood
on his dignity. One leg and a crutch
stood his ground on principles. It cost
him his job, it weighed him down with debts, but bought
in time, for us, the freedom of the press.
Bankrupt he visited this valley, 'Eildon'.

The party of kin he had led were settling well.

Six ruinous years in South Africa, that's all?
In London he became Secretary
to the Anti-Slavery Society.
When Coleridge declared 'Afar in the Desert'
to be 'the finest lyric in our tongue'
he was not convinced. No great poet,
he knew it, but hoped he might survive
in a line or two about our great heart-searching spaces?
The arks of animals we have shot?
The depths of racial loyalties and hates?

South African poets in English have so far failed
to find a path without his footprint on it;
and nowhere the slightest trace of a cripple's crutch ...

HANDS

Careless, I damaged my hand on the circular saw
deeply slicing the nail and flesh of the thumb
and cutting the index almost right through at the middle.
It was odd to see one's finger in section, half
off and hanging, almost detached. The Doctor did his best.
He sewed it on again. 'Hand surgery', he said,
'is major surgery. The thumb
will be OK in time, but that finger means
that you must stay in hospital for a while.'

After two days I knew it hadn't taken.
I could smell that bit of me was dead and going rotten.

Miasmic with sleep and drugs I saw again
a skilful primate use his hairy hands.
Boy I was, basking, waiting with a rifle
for dassies on the edge of Boesmans Krans.
I'd fallen into a doze, then woke aware
that I was not alone. The air was alive
with companionable chunterings. I opened an eye.

Almost surrounded I was by a numerous troop
of foraging baboons. A few yards away
a male with his left hand flipped a large stone over,
revealing a big, black, dancing scorpion,
with raised crab pincers open, tail curved up,
sting ready. A quick co-ordinated swoop:
the left hand nipped off the sting and the right
popped the little crustacean into his mouth.
He crunched it slowly like a delicious shrimp.

The Surgeon was a still, unhurried man
who kindly introduced me to my hand.
'We can save the thumb. We can save
the bottom half of the index finger.' That
was what I had hoped for, and nodded approval.
He said: 'But I don't think we should, it ought to go.
Do you mind if I go off at a seeming tangent?
In losing the top half of that finger you've lost
three or four million years of evolution.
The secret of the human hand goes back
to our ancestors in the trees. Most of the mammals
have paws with claws or pads to dig or scratch
while primates have hands and feet to clutch and catch,
fine instruments for grabbing and holding branches,
for dwellers in trees while picking and peeling fruit.
This all depends upon the opposition
of the thumb to the palm.' He seized the carafe to show me.
'Some primates, including our forebears, developed
a small refinement of immense importance:
pincers, precise, linked to the eye and the brain,
formed by the tip of the thumb and the index finger.
Few primates can do this.' And he showed me.
'Now, with your good hand, take this match from me.'
I did so. 'Now take this one, using your thumb
and your index below your knuckle.' It could be done,
but awkward. 'Now with your thumb and the tip of the second
finger.' No problem at all. He cleared his throat.
'That bit of index finger will be in the way.
If you agree I'll remove it, and its metacarpal,
then I will graft the muscles and veins and nerves

of the absent first to those of the second finger.
I'll reconstruct your hand so that the tip of your thumb
will meet the second fingertip exactly.'

He was as good as his word. Using the hand
I thank God for His and the surgeon's handiwork.
Of course I miss the circular saw, but how
to word my wonder at what we apes had learnt
before we could speak escapes me utterly.

GERIATRIC IN SPRING

When orchards and vineyards are pruned and plundered,
when birds have no songs nor flowers nectar for bees,
I wonder startled as a boy, I wondered
can leaves put flesh on skeletons like these?

Yet I indulge in a myth that underground
suckled on sap and warm among furry roots,
prides of emerald lions are licking wounds
or sniffing in sleep the first rain-sexy breeze.

Spring still startles me. Tight black buds shoot
pink and green claws to tear blue sky, and soon
each naked shape's attired, quite transformed
by foaming leaf and bloom.

                        No autumn sun
will bless my year with sweet predictable fruit.
Through me far different seasons shone and stormed.

THE ACORN MAN

Some years ago, the ageing Professor of English,
returning from reading the *King Lear* analogues,
saw on the pavement corner outside his house
a black man on his hands and knees
raking acorns into a sack with his fingers;
his peppercorn hair showed white on his ebony skull.
Though the sight does not surprise (he comes each year
in his cast-off white man's clothes to gather this mast
for his pigs) the Professor looks at the image afresh.

In his *History of the World* Sir Walter Raleigh
Points to Nebuchadnezzar as the type
of the proud king who learnt humility:
a fine great man, no mere tyrant, but one
with creative imagination, who remembered
his dreams and inquired what on earth they meant–
those golden-headed images with feet of clay,
gigantic trees felled to the ground, uprooted –
but failed, like Lear, to listen to their warnings,
went mad, abandoned shelter and clothes, on all fours browsed
on grass like a beast of the field – so the story went.
Seven years of penance among the beasts restored
his wits, and with humility enough to accept
the godship of his God: a notable conversion
which in due course earned him a special place
with Virgil and the Sybil as one of the three
pagan prophets of the Messiah's coming.

This old man is neither royal nor mad.
Crossing the road the Professor says, 'Good morning.
It's acorn time again.' 'Yes, oubaas.'
He gets up with a guttural cough. 'Master sees I am filling
these pockets with acorns,' and
he coughs again. They are near a bench. It's marked
Europeans Only. The Professor sits
and, gesturing with his hand, says, 'Sit.'

The old man hesitates. The Professor repeats,
'Please sit.' Dusting his knees, the old man sits.

'Are you still living in the township with
the S A Tuberculosis Association?'
'That is so.' 'You must ask them to X-ray your chest.'
He shrugs, and smiles, and coughs, 'X-rays always.'
'Where do you keep your pig, at SANTA?' 'No,
my pig is with my daughter. She lives there
by Manley's Flats, on Master Randall's farm.'
'Did you work there?' The old face frowns and smiles.
'Everywhere.' Born Salem, then Lombard's Post,
working with stock and pines, good years, bad years
down mines; this cough, the death of his good wife,
but, thank Thixo, their only child, their daughter,
bears almost every second year.

Each year he visits her at acorn time.
They were the best days of the year for him.
The children welcome him because of acorns.
Each day he gives each child a double handful
to ration the jubilant piglets. Now that
was a thing to see! That an acorn can make a child
so happy! He held one up, still in its cup.
'A small child likes to make a piglet happy.
And an acorn, a child and a small pig can make my daughter
and me so happy. Au!' The academic
has seldom seen anticipation so
illuminate a face. Then the cough
shakes him and the bench. 'How do you get those pockets
to the farm?' He joins his hands as if in prayer.
His voice is soft with deference. 'That gate
goes into master's garden?' 'That is so.'
'Master, it's far to carry sacks to SANTA.
At acorn falling can I put my pockets
just inside your gate? A few days only.
The donkey cart will come next week and take
them out to Manley's Flats.'

So that was agreed.
Apart from greetings they never talked again,
but once each year the Professor would watch a small
pyramid of pockets full of acorns
grow in his garden, then suddenly not be there.

A year-long fellowship took him and his wife
to the northern hemisphere, into a swing
of the seasons where no one takes for granted
an old man on his knees when the acorns fall.

Returning, among the pending mail he found
a barely literate letter with a blank address
from someone who'd walked out of SANTA because he said
he was getting no better; whose pension had not come;
who needs money now to redeem his impounded pig,
who is pregnant. Authorities at SANTA say
he left no address. Welfare can tell him nothing.
The farmer thinks he's got the wrong address.
Yes, there was a woman with a pig,
but she's left, he thinks, for family in the Kei.

The acorns are falling ungathered. Returning from work
each day, he recalls an old man on his knees,
not Nebuchadnezzar nor Lear, but his countryman,
a dignified old man with a talent for joy
who for years had done him the honour of using his garden
as a depot for his acorns. He picks one up,
still in its cup. 'O! I have ta'en
too little care of this.'

GRAVES OF HEISIB AND ISIVIVANE
for Douglas Livingstone

A poet friend and I were poring over
maps. Also accounts by early travellers,
engravings, and old photographs
of naked piles of undressed stones on the veld.
The Khoikhoi called them graves of Heisib
their god who is buried but never forever.
Sites for little rites of passage, halts
at crossroads, river fords, or water sheds
at which for how many hundreds of years
what hosts of mortals each paused to add a stone,

a sprig of green, a morsel of meat,
a ritual but personal plea.

Also at beginnings and endings to journeys,
an iron-smelting site at Broederstroom
a source of water in Damaraland
a farm close by to us, 'Ballinafad'.
The Nguni call them isivivane,
good places to pray in a reckless world.

The telephone rang in the other, the empty room.
Annoyed beyond reason I rose to answer it:
'Douglas Livingstone died last night.'
Some stumbling questions, few informative answers,
needed but nowhere near the point.
Douglas dead. No Douglas.

I put the mouthpiece down. I took three steps,
then stopped. Framed in the doorway ahead of me,
sat my friend and his, still in a world
where Douglas Livingstone was not yet dead.
As if in wartime I broke the news.
Maps go suddenly out of date.

***

Douglas had taken the immemorial routes
that always are new for each; at cairns of choice
casting a customary twig as if in passing,
some seemingly ordinary thing, a stone
ready to hand to lend its weight
to wishes that rang like a prayer.

But, on fresh frontiers with no cairns, he haunted.
There, gathering quite particular pebbles with love
and branches of aromatic shrubs he'd build
his cairns. We meet them. No epitaphs. They sing:
Douglas Livingstone, Giovanni Jacopo
practised his precious craft just here.

BELLOWING HIPPOPOTAMUS
Blue faience, Egypt 1600 BC, British Museum

Ancient Gyppo
loud-mouthed hippo
of blue faience

from what dark tomb
ridiculous
Lazarus
you've come
to bellow down our doom.

Unlike Eliot
world-weary that a wheel should turn
you do not
yawn
at dawn
nor grind out flinty blues
like Peat Heaney or Hawk Hughes.

Your belly-head shouts
life sans end
raises
pristine praises
like my friend
Clouts.

MALUS FLORIBUNDUS

Our wedding reception was held in your mother's garden.
Among its shrubs none lovelier nor more generous
than *Malus Floribundus.*

Fifty years later, the tree outside our kitchen window,
close to the stone of the work-shop wall, is repeating
its annual miracle. At the sun's touch

the deep roots' cold conspiracy with naked branches
has burst into the open
with millions of pink-tipped buds proclaiming the white
incoming tides of spring; week after week its blossoms
emit the zoom and burr of bees. *Floribundus*,
the day being warm, we sip our coffee in your shade.

When, after a decade of war, bitter *wanderjahre*,
we bought this nineteenth-century ruin of an inn
whose garden needed as much attention as the house,
you gave the local florist an order which included
Malus Floribundus. Three times he sent the wrong plant,
three times you plucked it up by its young roots. At last
the blossom was right. The young tree grew and grew
while we transformed the ruin into a home, while we
changed a waste into a garden, planting lemon and rose,
this tree grew up with our family, providing in time
a fine umbrella for the prams, the go-carts and the trikes.

How still and quiet it is. Remember their cries
of delight at the rainbow-coloured clothes you made them?

Now all have gone their far and individual ways.

Ours was a war-time wedding, white was not in vogue,
your dress was a delicate shade of green, simple, short,
and your hat sat saucily on the side of your golden head.

A sudden slight gust of wind creates such a swirling of petals
that I grope for a metaphor, 'a swarm of white-winged bees –'
but you, quite simply, correctly, say, 'Confetti.'

A BEE

The old man in the early light is pleased to hear
the shy Cape Robin tentatively tuning his voice for full
matutinal song. A thud from the nursery. It means

his grandchild's rejection of the empty bottle. It means
his own matutinal noises. Soon they will rise to a pitch
that will waken his parents at least an hour too soon.

The old man knows what to do: take the child for a walk,
by walking, the child can amaze himself and his parents
that he can stop crawling on four, can manage on two,
now *homo erectus* at last, both hands free, neck straight
and his whole view of the world subdued by the raising of his
                                                      eyes.
Child to his hip, he tiptoes down to the old, walled garden,
and slips him on the path to the gate. Progress is slow, each step
a daring decision, fists wide apart, an acrobat's balancing pole.
He gazes at who-knows-what of plants:
volumes of bougainvillaea, splashes of jacaranda
spilling over the old stone wall and its weathered gate.

The child looks up, asking for more. The gate is opened.
He stares through a sudden square into the sunlit street,
into that world without a wall. It's far too early
for traffic of any kind: not a soul about,
sunrise on leaves, blinding every drop of dew
on grass and weeds that green the tarmac verges: no sounds,
except the no-longer-shy Cape Robin's aria,
a heavy-duty truck dim on the distant national road.

It is really a trifle miraculous, the old man thinks,
that I and this child should be here at all. A common thought,
but these deep clichés often take me by surprise.

The child's gone down on his hunkers, the angle of his head
says that his eyes have been caught by something upon the earth.
There is such intensity in this act of looking,
that the old man freezes like a frightened buck, then slowly
adjusts his still top half to catch what has caught the child.
A daisy, a common golden Gazania,
family *Compositae*. Not rare at all,
but this one here is the first and only one these eyes
have seen. He rejects the itch to look at his watch to time
his span of attention.

From outer space a winged zoom
makes a six-point landing on the black air strip
that stripes each petal, and heads for the central forest of florets.
The whole flower shakes, then steadies itself, six legs scramble,
the hind pair yellows with pollen as the quick head ducks,
and dips, and dives, looting the hidden caches of nectar.

Of course, there are millions of hives. That polity
reached perfection ninety million years ago.
He censures himself for deadening generalities.
This is the only bee this pair of eyes has seen.

The child has turned his head, is looking straight at him,
gesturing with his hands to show this giant shadow
who's always showing him, this.
The old man gets down on his creaking hunkers
and looks for once at the common business of a bee.
For a period not to be measured by microchips
two generations of eyes are staring at what is there;
they've escaped the realm of clocks; it is not boredom
but the ache in his thighs that causes the elder to rise.

Just as he finds himself erect the bee zooms off
and the child, finding it gone, totters upright
looking into his eyes with a question: What next?

The old man dangles an enormous hand, the child
selects the index finger to enfold in a chubby fist,
and starts to walk, tugging, seemingly haphazard,
a giant who knows he will not want for wonders
this hour, with this guide.

A BAPTISM

for Judith and Caitlin

I stand near the font with my wife,
my son, his wife, and their daughter,
and others who think there's another life,
and a priest who is blessing the water.

I've come to this service believing
it has something to do with heaven.
Man hears the earth he is steadily leaving
quite clearly at seventy-seven.

The traffic outside reminds me
of time's black rolling stream,
but nothing on earth can ever blind me
to love's surprising gleam.

The time for the writing of verses
for those whom we love is over?
Outside this church waits a queue of black hearses
for the parent, the child and the lover?

I wrote a song for this son,
and many for his mother,
and others done, and some not done,
for a brother, a sister, a brother,

but for this girl and the child
she has given to us and the earth
my words, if they come, will be sober and wild
with the joy of newness and birth.

I look at my wife with wonder
at our son, his wife, and their daughter.
Whatever the threat in the sinister thunder
there's the gleam in this blessing by water.

NOTES

PILGRIMAGE TO DIAS CROSS (PAGE 223)

I *Cry! What shall I cry?* Isaiah 40:6. The whole chapter is relevant.

Laocoön. A Trojan priest who tried in vain to dissuade his countrymen from drawing into their city the 'Wooden Horse'. As Laocoön was preparing a sacrifice to Neptune, two huge snakes swam out of the sea, coiled round him and his two sons, and destroyed them.

II *Pilgrimage.* See V W Turner, 'Death and the Dead in the Pilgrimage Process' in *Religion and Social Change in Southern Africa: Anthropological Essays in Honour of Monica Wilson*, ed. M Whisson and M West (Cape Town, David Philip, 1975):

'Pilgrimages ... are full of symbols and metaphors for death, and are also directly concerned with the dead. The dead may include the founder of a religion, his kin, disciples or companions, saints and martyrs of the faith, and the souls of the ordinary faithful ... both pilgrims and initiands are undergoing a separation from a relatively fixed state of life and social status and are passing into a liminal or threshold phase and condition for which none of the rules and few of the experiences of their previous existence had prepared them.' (p. 107.)

'Structural distance may, then, be an apt symbol for death; the dissolution of distance, rebirth into authentic social life. They may see the move away as an opportunity for a direct, immediate confrontation of others as total human beings, no longer as segments or facets of a structured system ... Moreover, even the most harmoniously articulated structures in any culture produce some degree of "alienation", for the fullness of an individual's being overflows the totality of his roles and statuses.' (p. 109.)

III *Dias.* See *Dictionary of South African Biography*. 1:241; Eric Axelson, *Congo to Cape: Early Portuguese Explorers*, ed. George Woodcock (London, Faber, 1973).

IV *City of God.* Theopolis, a mission station, founded in 1814 by a number of Khoi (including Boesak) under the supervision of G Ullbricht of the London Missionary Society, on land granted by the Governor Sir John Cradock. In 1821 it passed into the care of George Barker. In spite of disputes about the land, it formed the one secure spot for the Khoi in the region. In 1829 about one hundred families were removed to the Neutral Territory – in fact the inheritance of

Maqomo, the terrain from which Ntsikana came. Theopolis was regarded by some as a hotbed of sedition, and was closed down after various skirmishes in 1852 at the time of the Hottentot Rebellion.

See Marion Currie, *The History of Theopolis Mission* (M A thesis, Rhodes University, 1983).

Boesak. Information about Cobus Boesak (not to be confused with the remarkable Boezak in *D.S.A.B.* IV:36) is hard to come by. Our main source for his role in the battle is C L Stretch, 'Makana and the Attack on Grahamstown in 1819', *Cape Monthly Magazine XII*, 1876, p. 301.

'At this critical moment ... the Hottentot Captain Boezac, with one hundred and thirty of his people, rushed intrepidly forward ... Boezac and his followers, some of the best marksmen in the country, levelled in a few minutes a number of the most distinguished chiefs and warriors ... Boezac, however, rushing intrepidly forward on the flank ... contributed considerably to the panic and defeat that followed.'

B Maclennan, *A Proper Degree of Terror* (Johannesburg, Ravan Press, 1986, p. 195) tells us that 'many years before, [Cobus] had undergone a difficult conversion to Christianity. As he explained to one of the Bethelsdorp missionaries in one of his rare sober moments, he had two hearts. The one heart would "do nothing but sing all kinds of Hottentots' and Bushmen's songs and all that is bad, and the other heart strives to sing the praises of Christ". At last the victory came, and filled with the love of Christ, Boezak laboured in and out of season in the cause of Christ.' Barker's diary says Boesak prayed better than anyone else; Barker also had to reprimand him for selling ivory to innkeepers and traders instead of bringing it back to the mission station. See references to Boesak and ivory-trading in *The Reminiscences of Thomas Stubbs*, ed. W Maxwell and R McGeogh (Cape Town, Balkema, 1978).

... once Men-of-men, we dwindled into middlemen. See Monica Wilson, *The Interpreters* (Grahamstown, 1820 Foundation, Dugmore Memorial Lecture, 1972).

Colonel Willshire. See *D.S.A.B.* I: 849.

Makandla. See Nxele, *D.S.A.B.* I: 596.

V   *Jeremiah.* Goldswain, Jeremiah. *D.S.A.B.* III: 333. His *Chronicle*, ed. Una Long (Cape Town, Van Riebeeck Society, 2 vols, 1946 & 1949) is one of the best first-hand accounts of the settlement in Albany. For the conflict in Wait's party see vol I, p. 23.

VI   *Karel Landman. D.S.A.B.* III: 496.
     Sekonyela. D.S.A.B. II: 648.
     Matiwane. D.S.A.B. I: 523.

VII *Nongqawuse. D.S.A.B.* I: 593.

Ntsikana. D.S.A.B. I: 595.

Enoch Sontonga. Enoch Sontonga came from the Mpinga clan among the Tembu. He worked as a teacher in a Methodist mission school at Klipspruit (Nancefield) near Johannesburg. He composed many songs and hymns in tonic sol-fa, nearly all of which have been lost. 'Nkosi Sikelel' iAfrika' was composed in 1897, seven more stanzas being added by S E K. Mqhayi. D D T Jabavu, writing in 1934 in an edition of the hymn published by Lovedale, said that it had been tacitly accepted as the national anthem of black South Africans. The ANC adopted it as the closing anthem of their meetings. The full version appeared in the *Presbyterian Xhosa Hymn Book* in 1927 (Lovedale Press).

Mqhayi. D.S.A.B. I: 565.

VIII *James Butler*. His diary, *Jim's Journals*, edited by Jane Garner, has appeared in the Grahamstown Series published by the University of Witwatersrand Press, 1997. James Butler (1854–1923), a Quaker, was educated at Croydon Friends' School and apprenticed to his father, a London watchmaker. At the age of 22 he was sent to South Africa, having contracted pulmonary tuberculosis. During his first visit he wrote *Jim's Journals*, letters home in diary form, filled with anecdote and comment. He spent some time with the Shaws of 'Richmond', striking up a deep friendship with the son, William Abercrombie.

William's tragic death (16 March 1878) left James with little doubt about the dangers of the country. The dry climate, however, was restoring his health.

In 1879 he established a general-dealers' shop in Cradock, then a bookshop, and in 1891 a newspaper, *The Midland News and Karoo Farmer*, which he edited until his death in 1923. It gained a reputation for fast and accurate news coverage. Its pacifist principles, however, were not popular during either the Anglo-Boer War or the First World War. He insisted that the enemy was human. He was one of those instrumental in getting a conscience clause included in the Defence Act (No. 13 of 1912, section 82 (2)). After his death he was acclaimed for his integrity as an editor and his efforts to reconcile English and Afrikaans-speaking South Africans.

In 1882 he married Annie Letitia, the eldest daughter of John Collett of 'Grassridge', himself the son of a settler, James Lydford Collett. James and Letitia had two sons and five daughters.

IX Moonrise on the 500th anniversary of planting the padrão occurred shortly after midnight.

XII *llha da Cruz*. St Croix Island.

Ilheus Chaos. Bird Islands.

Rio de Infante. The evidence seems to favour the Keiskamma River rather than the Fish.

... *signatures for our King*. 'Pacheco Pereira ... described how, five leagues beyond the Angra da Roco (Algoa Bay), was an islet just over half a league from the shore, on which Dias placed a padrão a little taller than a man with a cross on top of it and a triple inscription in Latin, Arabic and Portuguese, declaring that in the year of Our Lord Jesus Christ 1488 (and in so many years after the creation of the world) King João ordered Bartolomeu Dias, Captain of his ships, to discover this coast.' Dias in *D.S.A.B.*

One of our belated chroniclers. Barros, quoted by Axelson.

... *another chronicle*. See A Teixeira da Moto, *Bartolomeu Dias Discoverer of Cape of Good Hope*, translated by Luiz Marques (Lisbon, 1955), p. 18.

XIV *Heisib's grave*. Heisib, or Heitsi Eibib, is a semi-divine prophet and hero of the Khoi and San. He is killed and buried in many places, but he always comes to life again. His grave cairns are frequently at the entry to dangerous mountain defiles or river crossings. Travellers place a stone wrapped in grass, or small offerings of beer or honey, on them and say a prayer for good fortune on their journey. The custom was taken over by the blacks, who call such cairns Isivivane.

Guide me, O thou great Redeemer. A 'pilgrim' hymn much loved by settlers and their descendants, *Hymns Ancient and Modern* 397.

If I take the wings of the morning. From Psalm 93. I imagine this being sung in the rhymed Dutch version.

He who is our blanket of comfort. From Ntsikana's Great Hymn. For a full version see Janet Hodgson, *Ntsikana's Great Hymn* (UCT, Centre for African Studies Communications No. 4, 1980). The first translation into English (by John Brownlee) was published by Thomas Pringle in the *New Monthly Magazine*, 1827 (Hodgson, p. 6).

XVI *Sele! sele! /Ahom, ahom, ahom*. The 'Bell Song' of Ntsikana, 'Intsimbi Ka Ntsikana' (see Hodgson, p. 6). There is an ironstone boulder on a hilltop near Ntsikana's grave, which according to tradition he used as a bell, striking it with a small stone. Local inhabitants know the spot well. I was given a demonstration of the tune he struck from this 'bell'.

The quoted lines have no 'meaning'. In the final stanza they are followed by:

Sabelani, sabelani,
Niyabizwa ezulwini!

Ahom, ahom, ahom, ahom, ahom!
(Respond ye! respond ye!
to this call that comes from heaven!
Ahom, ahom, ahom, ahom, ahom!)

ODE TO DEAD FRIENDS (PAGE 246)

A few biographical details about the four friends to each of whom I devote a stanza:

1. Uys Krige, b. Swellendam 1910, d. Onrus 1987. Afrikaans poet and dramatist; proficient in several languages, and a superb translator into Afrikaans of Shakespeare and Spanish poets; inexhaustibly eloquent, and with a wonderful sense of humour.

2. Sydney Clouts, b. Cape Town 1926, d. London 1982. Considered by many as our most original poet. An opponent of all theories of literature or society which deprive the poet of his creative originality. Philosophers, of whatever school, belong to a secondary order. He died in exile in London. The headstone of his grave has Devil's Peak, Table Mountain, and Lion's Head in bas-relief upon it.

3. Professor Monica Wilson, b. Lovedale 1908, d. Hogsback 1982. Distinguished anthropologist, and responsible, with Leonard Thompson, for revolutionising the writing of South African history. Born of missionary stock, and educated at Lovedale when that great school was open to all, she had a rare understanding of African life. She was a great lover of plants, particularly trees. My wife and I used to visit her early in each year at Hogsback.

4. Matthew Goniwe, b. Cradock 1947, assassinated near Port Elizabeth 1985. An African school teacher and determined campaigner for improvements not only in education but in the lot of his people. He was imprisoned for three years under the Suppression of Communism Act. While serving his sentence in Umtata jail, he wrote to me asking for advice about writing poetry. Our correspondence developed into a friendship, which our meeting after his release confirmed. Details of his assassination, with three other activists, emerged in the hearings of the Truth and Reconciliation Commission.